MAGG

IN POLYGAMY'S SHADOW

From a Mormon Childhood to a Life of Choice

PUBLISHED BY JKS PUBLISHING

ISBN 978-0-9949288-0-1

Library and Archives Canada Cataloguing in Publication

Rayner, Maggie, 1949-, author
In polygamy's shadow : from a Mormon childhood to a life of choice
/ Maggie Rayner.

Issued in print and electronic formats.
ISBN 978-0-9949288-0-1 (paperback).--ISBN 978-0-9949288-1-8 (epub)

1. Rayner, Maggie, 1949-. 2. Rayner, Maggie, 1949- --Family.
3. Polygamy--British Columbia. 4. Mormon children--British Columbia--
Biography. 5. Mormon children--Family relationships--British Columbia.
6. Parent and child--Religious aspects--Mormon Church. 7. Mormon
families--British Columbia--Biography. I. Title.

BX8643.F3R39 2015   306.874088'2893   C2015-907175-5
                                            C2015-907176-3

Editor: Joyce Gram
Cover design: Simon Avery
Text design: Kelly Lee Parry
Printed by IngramSpark

Printed and bound in the United States.

JKS PUBLISHING EDITION, 2015
Published by JKS Publishing
#192-71 West 2nd Avenue, Vancouver, BC V5Y 0J7
www.maggierayner.com

Author's Note

This book is a memoir. It is a true story according to my best recollections, given the inevitable flaws of memory.

I have chosen to publish my memoir under my pen name rather than my family name. The names of my family, and the names and identifying characteristics of friends and other people mentioned in my story, have been changed to protect their privacy. Places and locations remain the same. In some instances, I've compressed events and time periods in service of the narrative. Otherwise, this is a true and honest account, and I have not knowingly misrepresented any material facts.

For my children,
who received Mormon tapes in the mail
instead of loving grandparents in their lives

Contents

IN POLYGAMY'S SHADOW

Introduction

I LIVED A LIE to stay safe. My parents were members of the Church of Jesus Christ of Latter-day Saints, commonly known as the LDS or Mormon church, founded in the 1800s by Joseph Smith.

The church portrays Mormonism as smiling families, with sparkling white teeth, living in Utah. Disillusioned members describe the church as a birthday cake filled with maggots. Those outside the faith consider the founder, Joseph Smith, to be—at the very least— a charlatan, a sex addict, and a pedophile. After Smith started his new church, he committed adultery with a young girl living in his home, who became pregnant. He framed his moral lapse as spiritual wifery, and opened the floodgates for his sexual appetites and those of his male followers. Under the auspices of plural marriage, or polygyny (one man having multiple wives), commonly known as polygamy, women became commodities to be traded. Their children were schooled to carry on Smith's religious rituals. The bonds of the family unit were weakened or rendered nonexistent. Loyalty to church over family continued after Smith's death. In the opening years of my life, in the 1950s and 60s, my parents placed the needs of the church above the needs of our family.

From my earliest memory, the limitations imposed on me by the church and by my parents were: don't think, don't feel, don't question. My activities and friendships were monitored. The books I read were censored. The daily mantra was: accept, obey, and take your preordained place in the patriarchal order. The threat of violence from my father, a highly respected church leader, rendered me an unwilling participant in the faith.

I fled home at eighteen to a shared house of non-Mormon

1

young women, and an entry-level office job in the city. I moved less than ten miles from home, yet it was as if I had entered a foreign country without a map or guidebook. For eighteen years, my life had been defined by the parameters of the religion. There were rigid rules about alcohol and tobacco, caffeine, clothing, music, entertainment, sex, how often to attend services, how much money to give in tithing and donations, and whom to socialize with.

Individuals' decisions about whether or not to follow these rules were unacceptable. Church leaders defined purity and goodness. The world outside their influence was considered evil. Men had absolute authority over their wives and children. Dysfunctional family systems flourished, including the one in my family. Both my parents were emotionally and intellectually immature, governed by their fear of an unforgiving Mormon god and the authority of their church leaders. Their lives were church-centered, and they were dependent on it.

Anytime I expressed an opinion or desire that conflicted with LDS doctrine, I was stamped down by my mother, and if he heard, by my father. My parents blindly obeyed the church. Through its eyes, and those of my parents, there was something wrong with me. I was flawed. Whenever I told my mother that I didn't want to go to services she admonished: "That's Lucifer talking, not you. He's a trickster, lying in wait to trip you up and get you to turn your back on your Heavenly Father, any way he can." I didn't buy it. Yet I had no choice but to live it.

I've been asked why, of the seven surviving children in my family, I was the only one who protested. Both my sisters were married in the Mormon temple. On graduating from high school, my oldest and youngest brothers served church missions, and they, too, had temple weddings. I don't have a definitive explanation for my resistance to Mormonism. My mother didn't welcome my birth? I learned early that I couldn't trust either of my parents, and that my mother lied to me? I was smarter than my siblings? Take your pick.

In 2011, the leader of the polygamous Mormon community in Bountiful, British Columbia, was in the news for tax fraud. My sympathies were with the children and young girls of Bountiful. I understood, from my childhood experience, why there was no need for barbed wire or metal bars to keep them contained and submissive. Indoctrination, isolation, and continuous pregnancies were sufficient. Their ongoing plight motivated me to write the article, "Polygamy and Me: Growing Up Mormon," published in the *Vancouver Sun*. I wrote about my polygamous ancestors and my parents' belief that they would live the principle of plural marriage in the afterlife. I wrote about my exposure to polygamy as an adolescent. And I wrote about my belief that Mormonism is a crock.

Reader response surprised me. What was so familiar to me, although a part of my life that I'd hidden, initiated a deluge of questions. I squirmed under the scrutiny, grappling with embarrassment about having revealed what I'd kept secret and was a source of shame. Everyone who approached me about the article wanted to know more about my Mormon upbringing.

The dam that I'd built to contain my childhood experiences began to crumble, then burst. I sat back down at my laptop. Two questions surfaced. Would a baby brother have lived if my father had taken him to a doctor instead of insisting that a church blessing would heal him? And did my overburdened and depressed mother purposely try to drown my sister and me? As an adult, I can only guess at the answers. As a child, in survival mode, these questions never occurred to me. They were simply confusing and traumatic events among the many that I knew of in my family, or lived through without choice. I present them as examples of the environment I was raised in, and the only world I knew.

My intent in writing my memoir is to answer the questions I've been asked about the practices of the religion I experienced growing up and my responses to them. I also write as a cautionary tale to anyone who is considering the religion, and as a testament to those leaving or who have already left. Readers desiring to compare LDS scripture with Christianity, to review the DNA evidence refuting Smith's claims, or to get updates on supposed Mormon prophecies since my childhood, can find information online. Much of what I write about is not acknowledged by the church or any of its members. Secrecy and denial are a necessary part of practicing the faith.

Mormon history and practices have been edited by the church to attract new members. Anyone investigating the faith is embraced by a nurturing social network, with the message of families first. After baptism, converts are gently encouraged to align their choice of friends, how they spend their time and money, and their family life with the mores of the congregation. The pretense of love is the lock on an invisible prison. LDS public relations grind out the slogan, "More people than ever are joining today." Yet the online forums of members raised in the faith—those that are leaving—tell a different story. Pain and grief pour from their posts. Their words weep with betrayal and loss as they navigate the maze ahead: on their own, often without family. The average person takes for granted the basic beliefs and skills that those who renounce the faith must master: understanding what personal needs are and their entitlement to them, dreaming their own dreams, and believing they are possible. I traveled the road to personhood by trial and error, a consumer of self-help books and therapy. My heart goes out to those yet to follow. Leaving is only the beginning. Creating a life of independence and choice, from the inside out, is the journey.

Although I left the church, its impact on me, and on my children and granddaughters, remains. My mother sent Mormon tapes to my children in the mail, instead of being a loving presence in their lives. My children's birthdays and Christmases passed without notice from my mother and father. My children have no contact with their aunts and uncles or cousins. No loving or social bonds outside the church were formed. Life in my family was about church, not personal connection. My granddaughters have never met my brothers or sisters, or any of my nieces and nephews.

A few years ago, I had a conversation, or rather a non-conversation, with my eldest and best-loved brother, Rob, during an afternoon visit on one of his trips to British Columbia. At the time, he was a businessman and lived in a predominately Mormon town in southern Idaho. I saw him every ten years or so, for a few hours. Seven years older, he had always been kind and caring, and a surrogate father to me in my childhood.

"When it comes to financial investments," he told me that afternoon over lunch, "the church advises us that we should . . ." Stunned, my immediate thought was, *What do you think?* Yet I stayed quiet, afraid to speak, reverting to the behavior of my childhood. If I'd been the person I am today, rather than the made-up, voiceless person I was as a child and that he knew, would he still love me? Would I ever see him again? I couldn't risk it.

I chose the name Maggie Rayner as a pen name to allow me, safely and freely, to write my thoughts and feelings about the Mormon church and my family. While I refer to myself as Maggie in my memoir, that wasn't my name at the time. Most people today know me as Maggie, a woman who bears no resemblance to the person I once was, chained by another name to a past that offered no hope of emotional wholeness or happiness.

Genesis

DAD'S GRANDFATHER JOHN was a polygamist. His two wives each had their own home. Lillian, wife number one, lived on a homestead near the railroad stop at the north end of Cardston, in southern Alberta. Martha, wife number two, lived in a wood-framed house with a piano in her parlor, close to the center of Cardston.

My great-grandfather John and his wives were Mormon, living the tenet of plural marriage that Joseph Smith had introduced to his church membership. Smith officially married forty-nine women in ten years. Historical researchers reference additional unions. With many of his wives wed to other men when he married them, any children he fathered could be explained. If an abortion was necessary, a Mormon doctor in his circle of cronies complied. Right to his death, Smith publicly denied his practice of spiritual wifery. The leader who succeeded him married fifty-five wives, some he had swapped with Smith.

Polygamy was denounced by the church at the turn of the twentieth century in order to gain statehood for Utah, the Mormon enclave. Privately, plural marriage in the church continued into the 1920s. The leaders told the membership that polygamy had only been suspended and would resume in the afterlife.

According to the faith's doctrine, after his death a man will become a god, have multiple wives, and rule over countless worlds. He will enjoy the earthly pleasures of sex with multiple women for eternity. A woman will become one wife among many, subject to the law of her god-husband while bearing him spirit children to populate his worlds.

My parents were married in the LDS temple, the gateway to Mormon heaven, in Cardston, Alberta. They believed that the secret ceremony they participated in joined them, and any children they had, for all eternity. Mom at twenty-six and Dad at thirty-two may have been each other's last chance for marriage to a church partner. Their faith was all they had in common.

My mother's parents were wealthy farmers in a small, southern Alberta community. Her two siblings had already left home when she was born. A respected member of the church, my grandfather was notorious for his temper. He beat his sheepdog to death for herding his sheep past the farm gate. Mom often hid to escape his wrath. As a young woman, she worked as a secretary and earned more money than Dad.

Dad, the eldest of eleven, broke horses in the foothills nearby. He rode bareback into town on a half-broken gelding to court Mom. Before they married, Dad went on a two-year mission to the Texas-Louisiana mission field. He sold his horses to pay his way, cut his waist-length hair, and traded in his buckskin jacket and chaps for a suit. Mom waited.

During the marriage ceremony in the temple, they each committed their lives, their unborn children, and all their worldly goods and talents to the LDS church. They were promised in return that they would be a god and goddess, a king and queen, in heaven. Each swore a blood oath to defend the church with their life, drawing a hand across their throat and abdomen to mime having their throat slit and being disemboweled if they didn't.

The Mormon church, which devoured my ancestors and my parents, laid claim to me—body and soul—before I was conceived. Three ruled over me as a child: the church, my father, and on the lowest rung, my mother.

Complicated Sorrow – 2004

IT'S FIVE-THIRTY IN THE MORNING and pitch-black. My Toyota Tercel rattles across the loading ramp onto the Bowen Island ferry, headed for Horseshoe Bay on the mainland. The lights on the car deck dim and shadowy figures stumble up the stairs to the passenger lounge. I shiver in my Tercel and stay put. I don't want to talk to anyone.

I have no desire to visit Dad in the hospital in Penticton. On my last visit to his care home four years ago, I drove Mom over and counted the minutes till we were out of there. How much time does Dad have left? And how is Mom coping? It would have been so much easier for me to stay home. Go? Stay home? Argh! Which will I regret?

The surface of the Trans-Canada Highway east is icy. I take it slow. It's eight o'clock now and the sky shifts from black to gray. Not much of an improvement. Snow falls lightly at the lodge in Manning Park, my stop for coffee and breakfast halfway through the trip. My stomach is in knots. How will I feel when I see Dad? I *could* turn around and drive back home, no one's stopping me. I slurp the strong brew and choke down bacon and eggs without tasting them. I'm an adult now, with my own family, not a frightened child. Competent. Successful. People respect me. I pay the check with a twenty-dollar bill and don't wait for change.

Mom phoned yesterday and told me that Dad had been transferred, stricken with a flu virus, from his care home to a private room at Penticton Regional Hospital. At ninety-four his mind wanders, although his body has stayed strong. That was until he caught the flu. He and Mom are in separate care homes. Mom's mind is alert; only her body has deteriorated. She's sure to go on and on about the Mormon church. I'll keep my mouth shut, as always. She's upset enough already.

Close to the sprawling Okanagan town, Skaha Lake comes into view. The sun is sharp and the sky suddenly blue. Good thing I remembered my sunglasses. I drive straight to Trinity Care Home, take a few deep breaths, and go in. Mom is waiting for me in her room. As soon as I see her hunched over in her wheelchair, all I want to do is take care of her.

Outside, the dry air crackles with cold. I settle her and her wheelchair into my Tercel and drive the short distance to the hospital, careful not to jar her frail body. Her mouth is a tight line and her eyes blink away moisture. With the harsh smell of disinfectant filling my nose, I wheel her from the elevator through the hallway to Dad's room on the fourth floor.

Dad is unconscious. Harmless. An IV on a metal pole drips fluid into a vein in his hand. My stomach relaxes. "I'm sure you want time alone with him, Mom. I'll be back in a little while." Her eyes are liquid with pain. I pause in the doorway and glance back. Bent double with osteoporosis, Mom clasps the limp hand of the man she's been married to for sixty-three years. Her lips move, but no sound comes out. Maybe she's praying. At the end of the hallway, in the family room, I sink into one of the soft chairs, cradle my face in my hands, and weep.

Back at Trinity with Mom, her body appears smaller, more crumpled than when we left for the hospital. What is she thinking and feeling, knowing Dad will soon be gone? A nurse's aide bustles in to take care of her. At least she has the comfort of her belief in Mormon heaven, and her church family, for support. Hopefully, her church family will visit. I want her to be well taken care of even though I'm not able to do it.

I return to the hospital and sit beside Dad. He's still unconscious, but twists and turns and pushes the sheet and blanket away from his body. I gently pull both back in place. My chair semireclines, comfortable enough to doze half-sitting up. There's no longer any need for the caution around him that I never grew out of. He'll never erupt in anger against me again. I'm safe. I'm in the same room with Dad and I'm safe. He can't ever hurt me again.

Hour by hour my vigil slides by. The terror trapped inside me for decades drains away. Peacefulness takes its place. I visualize Dad as he was in my childhood, dark-haired and handsome, wearing a suit and tie and a crisp white shirt. He's smiling. In his hand is his briefcase, filled with books of scripture. I picture him at home in his jeans and cowboy hat, a different man. And I think of myself as a small child, trying to please him, vying for crumbs of attention. Is there anything I need to say to him before he dies?

As Dad lies unconscious, is there a part of him aware and hanging on in the hope that his six other children will visit? Does he know he's dying? I have no idea exactly what happens after death. I don't believe, as he did all his life, that there are multiple worlds waiting for him to rule over or women eager to bear him spiritual children. Dad's life as an obedient worker bee for the church has simply been in service to an 1800s testosterone-fueled fantasy of Joseph Smith's, a fantasy that enriches the corporate coffers of the Mormon church today.

I comfort myself with the belief that after death, a loving existence with no Mormon requirements waits. Spirituality is important to me, not religion. I believe in an afterlife filled with loving energy that we all have access to here on earth. Different words are used throughout the world to describe what I call God.

Occasionally, if I think about dying and the mystery of what happens after my spirit leaves my body, a chasm of fear cracks open and leaves me faint. Then certainty rushes in like a tide and washes through me. I'm convinced that there is something more. Something fluid, expansive, and loving that can't be defined in language the way organized religions do. Something impossible to comprehend through the narrow lens of humanness.

The dogma of Mormonism has spoiled me for opening myself to any authority other than myself to interpret spirituality or the afterlife. I've searched for answers in Buddhism, Wicca, and nondenominational churches and come up empty. I trust in a peace that passes all understanding, impossible to catalog, reached through a personal connection with universal loving energy. I experienced this peace as a child, when the forest and streams called to me and offered comfort, and when I gazed up at the endless night sky filled with stars. It speaks to my soul in the twilight state between dreaming and waking, and flows through my being when I quiet myself and ask.

Ten days after my vigil beside Dad in the hospital, I travel back to Penticton with my husband for Dad's funeral. On the ten-minute drive from our downtown motel to the Mormon chapel on South Main Street, the clock in our VW van starts ticking. The hair on my arms stands up. In eight years of owning this van, the hands on the clock have never budged. "Do you think he's here, trying to tell me something?" I whisper.

Is Dad's spirit directing the electromagnetic field of the clock? Has he kick-started it in an attempt to tell me something? If so, I have no idea what or whether I'm the only one he's trying to communicate with. As we drive, my eyes are riveted on the black metal arrows and the minuscule, steady progress of the minute hand. I've heard stories about clocks stopping, grandfather clocks chiming, and phonographs playing on their own after a death.

At the chapel, wall-to-wall people spill out the front doors onto the sidewalk in the frosty morning sun. We park in the rear lot and go in the back door. A cacophony of voices in the hallway and foyer roars in my ears. My oldest brother Rob and his wife Ann have picked up Mom and her wheelchair from Trinity Care Home, directly across the street from the church.

Dad's open coffin rests on a gurney in the women's Relief Society room used for informal gatherings. Members file past to pay their respects. We had a family showing at Everden Rust funeral home last night.

My husband and I join my siblings, all dressed in black, on one of the front pews in the chapel. I turn my head to check who's behind us, but don't recognize anyone. The air is heavy, as if filled with a sluggish fog. A complicated sorrow ambushes me. It rolls through me in waves, takes up residence, and makes it hard to breathe. I swallow and blink back tears. Am I grieving the loss of what I never received from Dad or the loss of my preschool adoration of him? My sister Sarah, beside me, reaches out and touches my arm. I keep my eyes on the podium.

The program has, of course, been arranged by my brothers, although my sisters and I are included. Rob and my youngest brother, Peter, the only practicing Mormons left among my siblings, sit at the front facing the congregation with the bishop (the ecclesiastical leader of the ward or congregation) and his two counselors. The bishop announces the opening song: "I Know that My Redeemer Lives." While the organ pumps out the prelude, I pick up the black book from the rack on the back of the pew in front of me and turn to page 136. The lyrics are familiar from my childhood, as if no time has passed: "I know that my Redeemer Lives. What comfort this sweet sentence gives . . ."

After an opening prayer by one of the Penticton congregation, Rob is the first of my brothers to speak. As my turn on the program gets closer, I start sweating. Will I be able to open my mouth? If only I had a bottle of water with me. Anything loving I have to say about Dad froze inside me after his beating when I was five. What can I say about the man who reduced me to an animal with his belt while he laughed and forced me to hit my sister? What can I say about the father I watched hurt my family in so many ways? The only redeeming thing I can think of is that when we lived in Gibsons, he bought his favorite maple walnut ice cream, in round two-and-a-half gallon tubs, for us kids, and yard-long boxes of cones.

For Mom's sake, now isn't the time to talk about my belief that the patriarchal Mormon church is a system that attracts, honors, and perpetuates generations of men similar to my father. Dad never talked about his childhood. My grandfather's treatment of Dad and his siblings had to have been a model for how Dad treated our family. It has carried on. I've seen my younger brother Michael knock his ten-year-old son from a chair to the floor, and I've heard the boy's screams as Michael beat him with his belt. How do my other brothers treat their children behind closed doors?

The one thing I have is Dad's journal from his missionary years, which Mom gave me. As I read it, I discovered a man with a grade eight education and poorly written grammar, who'd gone to agricultural college. He'd had some of his poetry published in the *Improvement Era*, a church publication. He'd yearned to be an airplane pilot, and his ambition was to research and write American archeology.

Instead, he put his desires on hold for eight years while he worked and sent money home to feed his ten brothers and sisters. I've never given much thought to Dad's life before he married Mom. Now I can't imagine that there was much happiness in it, other than his love of horses and the church. In his journal, he wrote of his life being stalled and his hope that serving a mission for the church would provide the answer. Some mornings, he was so depressed he had trouble getting out of bed.

In Salt Lake City, while at the mission home training to preach the gospel, he attended sessions at the temple, the highest place of worship in the Mormon faith. He was promised that if he committed his life to the church, he would become a god and king in heaven. After each session, he floated on the high he had experienced during the secret ceremonies, convinced that the euphoria he had felt was God witnessing the truthfulness of Joseph Smith's gospel to him.

My name is called to speak. I suck in my breath and squeeze past the knees of my siblings to the end of the pew. I walk up three short steps, stand behind the podium, and glance over the congregation of strangers. My body vibrates as I lay pages on the flat, wooden surface and grasp the edges for support. Face flaming, I swallow and introduce myself. My voice is hesitant, thready. Then, head down, I forget about other people and read for myself.

In 1937, my father served a mission for the church in the Texas-Louisiana mission field. He kept a diary while he was away. Mom entrusted his journal to me, and I consider myself to be the most fortunate of his children to hold it in safekeeping. In reading his daily writings, I met a man I never knew, and my life has been enriched as a result . . .

My talk fills the allotted five minutes, no more, no less. I move back to my seat, face still flushed, relieved it's over. My impersonal goodbye is for the man Dad was before he became my father. It contained no fond memories and no affection for my life with him. It's the best I can do for the man I can't honor as my parent, but whom the Mormon church holds in high esteem. My talk is for Mom. It's the price I'm willing to pay to please her, and to be a part of a family.

We Lived in a Tool Shed – 1950s

I STARED UP AT THE CEILING, my three-year-old eyes riveted on the globs of tar that sagged into tear drops. Splat! Down they came. Mom shrieked, "Clarence! Clarence!" She grabbed newspapers and sheets and tore around the room, throwing them on her piano and over our beds. Tar stuck to the table, the chairs, and the floor, its rank odor trapped in the heat. My nose stung.

Mom collapsed onto the only clean chair, covered her face with her hands, and sobbed. Her shoulders shook. Guttural sounds came out of her like an animal's, so harsh my stomach hurt as if I'd been punched hard. I wanted to say, "I'll wipe it up for you, Mom," but my mouth wouldn't open.

Dad came running. Mom screamed, "Look at all the extra work you've caused me. Do something." A logger, not a roofer, Dad had rolled black paper onto the top of our tool shed and spread tar over it to keep the rain out.

He surveyed the mess from the doorway, adjusted his cowboy hat, and laughed until his eyes were wet. "That must have been the wrong grade of tar for the roof. It was probably too old to use anyway. No wonder the highway guys gave it to me for free." Mom made strangled, mewling noises and cradled her pregnant belly. "Where's your sense of humor?" Dad asked. If he wanted to make her laugh, it didn't work. She kept on crying.

The roof, made of planks with the layer of paper and tar on top, had worked just fine over the fall and winter. But as the weather warmed up and the sun got hot during the day, the tar melted and seeped through the spaces in the planks. Dad and my brother Rob climbed up a ladder onto the roof and scraped as much of

17

the gooey mess off as they could. The drips dwindled to the occasional splotch.

We had moved to Gibsons on the west coast of British Columbia after Mom and Dad lost their farm in Alberta. Dad had arranged a job managing a sawmill. Rob was ten, my oldest sister Sarah nine, and my next sister Janice four. Dad bought the tool shed for us to live in at the auction after the high school was built. He moved it to the property he had purchased on Gower Point Road, in the shadow of a rock bluff close to the beach.

The shed was rectangular, with wide slats nailed to studs and tarpaper tacked onto the outside. Small windows set into the middle of each wall let in light. There was a door at each end. The inside was big enough for our round oak table, a chesterfield, and Mom's piano, which her parents had given her as a wedding present. Mom and Dad's bed fit behind a partition.

Dad built a lean-to room onto the back end where we kids slept. Then he added an extra bit of roof outside the kitchen door for Mom's wringer washer. We had a pot-bellied woodstove for heat, and Mom cooked on a Coleman camp stove. A tap with cold running water was outside the door by the washer. In the winter, our breath formed clouds in the house and we left our coats on. Mom hung wool blankets inside the two doors to keep the drafts out.

On the other side of the property was a proper house: with stucco, a real kitchen, a bathroom, and bedrooms. Dad owned it, and Aunt Winnifred and Uncle Ted, one of Dad's younger brothers, and my cousins Nonie and Jennifer, the same ages as Rob and Sarah, lived in it.

I never questioned the blankets inside our doorways in the winter or wondered why Nonie and Jennifer lived in the proper house Dad owned and rented to his brother while we live in a shed. To me, the tool shed was home. We called it "the little house around the bay."

If Mom minded that Aunt Winnifred lived in the proper house and she didn't, she never complained because Uncle Ted paid rent to Mom and Dad. Mom knew, as we kids did, that living in the tool shed was one of Dad's schemes to make money. "It's the only way to get ahead," he said. "Sure, we have to do without a few things and eat mush for a while, but it'll be worth it in the long run."

One-tenth of the rent money—and of any money my parents received—went straight to the church as tithing before Mom and Dad bought food for our family. Tithing is one of the requirements for a ticket into Mormon heaven and eternal salvation. I came to believe, years later, that the church took care of itself before the well-being of its members.

As Mom did endless chores throughout the day, she told us kids, over and over, "We're God's chosen people. We're special, the same as the pioneers who crossed the plains to the Salt Lake Valley in Utah. Mormonism is the only true religion on earth." Whenever she talked about the church, there was longing in her voice. "One day, we'll worship with a congregation again, every week, just as we did in Alberta."

The closest LDS congregation was an hour's ferry ride to Horseshoe Bay and another hour's car ride from there to Vancouver. A ferry trip was costly, and Mom and Dad could only afford to take us to services a few times a year. I hated sitting for hours on a hard pew. Every time I fidgeted, Mom scowled and pinched me. I never understood how she expected me to love the church as she did.

The first day of the tar drip—the worst day—we all got smudged with black stickiness. Mom bathed Janice and me in the laundry tub outside, scrubbing me till I was red and sore. After she lifted me out, I dropped my towel and jumped around, shaking my head back and forth to dry my short hair. As the summer heat danced on my bare skin, I wiggled and shook even faster.

"Stop that right now. Will you never learn? God wants you to be modest. Get your pajamas on." Mom sighed.

As she dried Janice off, Janice clung to the towel and kept herself covered while Mom helped her into her pajama bottoms. Janice gifted me with a smug smile that said, "This is how it's supposed to be done. What's the matter with you anyway?"

Rob and Sarah crossed to the proper house with towels, fresh underwear, and a bar of soap to have their baths. As soon as Sarah got back, she said to Mom, "Aunt Winnifred frowned at me and said don't you get any of that mucky tar on my clean floor. She never said anything to Rob." Sarah's voice trembled. Mom's lips tightened.

"Stop making a fuss. We have to put up with it for now."

Rob came back from his bath and mused, "It feels funny taking a bath in the house we own but other people live in."

"When our ship comes in, we'll have our own bathtub," Mom promised before she put Janice and me to bed. The lean-to where we slept was big enough for a small set of bunk beds and a single bed. There was a sliver of space down the middle. Janice and I slept head to toe in the bottom bunk, and Sarah slept in the top one. Rob had the single bed to himself.

Mom had to bend over to tuck the two of us in. The ceiling wasn't high enough for her to stand up straight. In bed, Janice and I pumped the bottoms of our feet together and giggled, pretending to have frog legs. "Stop that silliness if you want me to read to you." She opened a Babar book from the library van.

I didn't hear a word she read. I was thinking about Dad fixing the roof so Mom would be happy again. When Mom was mad at Dad, everything inside me shook. Then I thought about getting a bathtub so Sarah would never have to go over to Aunt Winnifred's for a bath again. It never occurred to me to want a bathtub for myself. I had already learned not to expect or ask for anything for myself.

Without

I WAS ALWAYS HUNGRY. We had boiled porridge in the morning, fried porridge for lunch, and broken-up pieces of bread soaked in milk from our cow Daisy for supper. Dad poured the yellow cream from the top of the bottle onto his bread. He was served first and got the best of everything. Macaroni or boiled dried beans were a treat. Beans were my favorite, and there were never enough. My stomach ached with hunger and screamed for more. I wasn't old enough to earn money to buy extra food, as Rob did with his paper route or Sarah by babysitting for neighbors. They didn't bring the food they bought home.

My friends Bobby and Brent, who lived up the street, often came outside with sandwiches in their hands. The smell of peanut butter spread on white, store-bought bread tortured me. Mom would complain, "Why that woman sends her children outside with food, I'll never know. No manners. No manners at all."

When it came to us doing without food, it wasn't that Dad was lazy. Dad worked at Mr. Pope's sawmill every day except Sunday— God didn't allow Mormons to work on the Sabbath. "Even though he's a Jew, he's not too bad to work for," Dad told Mom one evening. He stretched his legs on the chair beside him and rested one arm on the table. "A shame about his nose, though. There's not much left of it. That cancer's a filthy thing." He shook his head and clucked his tongue. "How he managed to get a second wife, and a young one at that, I can only guess."

"Hmmph." Mom raised her eyebrows. "It doesn't hurt that he's got money to buy her a fancy house and fancy clothes. I hear she doesn't even cook. And no children to take care of either." In

Mom's eyes, Mrs. Pope was selfish and spoiled. I was sure, though, that in her heart of hearts, Mom wanted exactly what Mrs. Pope had.

Mr. Pope's first wife was dead, and his second wife was younger than his son. Anytime she was mentioned, Rob would smile and snigger. I assumed this had something to do with what adults talked about. "Why are you smiling like that?" I asked him.

"When you're old enough, I'll tell you." He winked.

I only met Mr. Pope once, when Dad took me with him in the truck to pick up his paycheck. I couldn't stop staring at his nose, which was, just as Dad said, skin-colored plastic.

Mom cashed Dad's paycheck at the bank in Lower Gibsons. At home, she counted the money into piles and set aside one-tenth for the church. "We need the blessings we're promised by the prophet for paying tithing," she told Sarah, Janice, and me in her Sunday school lessons. Each Sunday morning, Mom read from a manual that church headquarters in Salt Lake City sent in the mail. We girls sat at the kitchen table with Mom while Dad gave Rob lessons behind Mom and Dad's bedroom partition. They kept their voices low. I knew they were talking about the priesthood, which was only for men. Mom would never describe in detail exactly what the priesthood was or answer my questions about why Rob was singled out to learn about it and we girls weren't. All she would say was, "When you're older, you'll understand the perfect order of God's plan." I never did, no matter how old I became.

The prophet Mom talked about in her Sunday school lessons was David O. McKay, the president of the church. God supposedly talked to him and gave him directions to relay to the membership. His picture appeared on the front of the church magazines *The Children's Friend* and *The Improvement Era*—an old man with wavy white hair.

A traveling grocery van from Vancouver stopped at the corner in front of the little house on Wednesday mornings at fifteen minutes after ten. The first time the van came over on the ferry, my eyes never left the kitchen clock. Mom, Janice, and I joined the small group of women and children waiting at the corner. On schedule, the van rumbled to a stop, double doors creaked open, and a set of metal stairs folded down to the ground. My mouth was dry as I climbed up the steps behind Mom and Janice. Inside the van were floor-to-ceiling shelves lined with food. Colored pictures of the contents were on each box and can. I wanted everything, especially Campbell's tomato soup and Christie's saltine crackers in the red box with the separate packets inside that I'd had at other people's houses. My stomach squeezed with desire. Mom bought yeast and sugar.

That night, as on other nights, I dreamed of candy bars and potato chips and money to buy any kind of food I wanted, especially the soup and crackers. The food and paper bills dangled from the branches of trees, just out of reach. Before we sat down to breakfast the next morning, I said to Mom, "Wouldn't it be wonderful if we could buy anything we wanted from the grocery van?"

"When our ship comes in, we'll have as much as we can eat. Store-bought bread and pretty dresses." After our ship came in, I would never have to wear worn-out boys' shirts or pants that had to be cinched in at the waist with a belt. I would be able to get a pair of sunglasses and white sandals with straps that left most of my feet bare. "Movie stars wear sunglasses and sandals," my friend Christine had told me one afternoon at her house, "and bright red lipstick on their lips. That's why they're so pretty."

The beach called to me and the ocean sang lullabies of joy and abundance as day after day I scanned the horizon for our ship. All that came ashore was the Landers' house on a barge. A bulldozer dragged it across the beach to its resting place on a foundation of creosote-blackened blocks, where it stood high in the air, its underside exposed and ugly.

At the end of the summer, I gave up my watch. Mom had lied. There was no ship. Everything she had told me was made up. None of it was true. She couldn't be trusted. All that I had hoped for and dreamed about, all that was important to me, was never going to happen.

"We have the church, that's what's really important," Mom said the afternoon I told her that I knew there was no ship. "We're building up riches in heaven. That's better than anything here on earth. The church says it's harder for a rich man to get into heaven than to thread a camel through the eye of a needle."

I had started to hate the church that Mom loved and talked about as if it were a living being. I could never say that to her. I was too afraid of what she would do to me. All I cared about was having a fancy dress, a pair of white sandals that would make me as beautiful as a movie star, and enough food to eat so I would never be hungry again.

Funerals

I DIDN'T WITNESS IT, I heard it—a squeal of tires followed by a mewling yelp, then silence. A car door slammed. I dashed from the woods at the back of the little house to find a small crowd of adults and kids gazing down at the pavement by a stopped car. I hung back. A squished mat of black fur lay beside the front tire with blood trickling into a pool on the asphalt.

Bobby whispered to me, "I think it's your cat, Mouser." He turned away while my other friends, Christine and Brent, sniffed back sobs. I began to choke. Mouser was an outside cat. Mom wouldn't let him inside, no matter how cold or wet it was.

I had asked Mom a number of times why Mouser couldn't come in. Every time she said, "We have too many children to have indoor pets. Back on the farm, cats live in the barn, *not* in the house." If Mouser didn't come when I called, I was always afraid that a coyote had eaten him or he had gone over the hill because I hadn't kept a close enough eye on him.

When our dog Spence went over the hill, Mom said it was because he wouldn't stop barking. Spence went with Dad and his rifle in the pickup truck, and when Dad came back Spence wasn't with him. In my heart I knew what had happened, but as long as I didn't ask, I could pretend it hadn't. No one talked about him again and a queasy ball of fear stayed curled in my stomach for weeks afterward.

"I'm so sorry." The elderly man who had run over Mouser blinked and glanced around. "I didn't notice the cat until it was too late. It ran right in front of my car." He shook his head and his voice trailed to a whisper. Mom stood beside me with her hand on my shoulder and glowered at him, her eyes narrow.

"The least you can do is move the cat off the road." Her voice was harsh.

The man got a newspaper from the front seat of his car, slid it gently under the squished matt of fur, and laid Mouser on the grass beside our driveway. I sat on a log beside him all afternoon, hoping to glimpse the white wisp that was Mouser's spirit drift up to the clouds into heaven.

Mom had told us in her Sunday school lessons that when Mormons died, their spirit went to the celestial kingdom, the highest of the three degrees in heaven. The second degree was the terrestrial kingdom, for people who were good but weren't Mormon. The third degree, the telestial kingdom, was for burglars and murderers. People who had seen Jesus Christ and denied him didn't get into any of the kingdoms but went instead to a place called outer darkness, where they suffered forever. I imagined that the celestial kingdom was a peaceful garden with a manicured lawn and flowers, where the sun shone every day, birds chirped, and butterflies flitted about.

"Earth is just the twinkling of an eye compared to heaven," Mom often told us. "Dying isn't anything to be unhappy about. A funeral should be a celebration. We Mormons are the lucky ones. God is waiting to welcome us. If people knew just how wonderful the celestial kingdom is compared to life here on earth, they'd kill themselves to get there."

Committing suicide didn't make any sense to me at the time. Mom's message, however, repeated often, slipped below the surface of my consciousness and lay dormant. Years later in times of crisis, the idea of suicide reached out its hand to taunt and comfort me.

I never caught sight of Mouser's spirit. I assumed that I'd been too late to see it or that perhaps he didn't have one. The Sunday school manual from Salt Lake City Mom read from never mentioned which of the kingdoms in heaven was for cats.

Hunting Down Horses

WHENEVER LOG DELIVERIES were late, Mr. Pope's sawmill shut down. Dad found odd jobs shoeing horses or clearing land with an old yellow bulldozer. Sometimes he went into town to buy calves to raise for sale as beef cattle. On one of the mornings that the mill was shut down, Mom said to him at breakfast, "Why don't you take Maggie with you to the Johnsons? I could do with a break."

I had fun going with Dad—as long as he let me get out of the pickup. Whenever he told me to wait in the cab, he said, "I'll only be a minute." His minute could drag out to hours. Often, by the time he opened his door I was asleep on the seat. Those times, he would shake his head and say in surprise, more to himself than to me, "I completely forgot I had you with me."

Mom never sent Janice with Dad. She took extra notice of her and kept her close. Janice was the first baby Mom had after my brother Tommy died at six months. When visitors came, Mom told them stories about all the cute things Janice did and how sensitive she was. "She needs to eat first thing in the morning or she's just plain miserable," or "Janice was so upset when her favorite dress caught on fire while it was drying next to the stove. You should have seen the horror on her poor little face." Mom never told anyone about Janice biting Sarah on the stomach. Sarah still has the scar.

Janice was special to Dad too. On his trips into Vancouver, he bought her dresses trimmed with lace. I imagined myself wearing each dress once she had grown out of it, although by the time she did, they were stained and torn.

At the Johnsons, Dad let me get out of the cab. He cautioned, "Horses are the same as people. If you treat them right, they'll treat you right. If they're spooked, they'll lash out at you faster than you can blink." As a teenager, Dad had had his nose broken by a kick from a green horse. That hadn't stopped him from loving horses. He was weak for them: mares, stallions, geldings, even workhorses like Clydesdales. The church wouldn't let Dad smoke cigarettes or drink coffee or liquor. He had to obey the church's Word of Wisdom, which meant no tobacco, no caffeine, and no alcohol. He wasn't allowed to play cards or gamble either. Horses were the one passion the church allowed him.

In the Johnsons' barn, he held each horse's bridle and murmured soothing sounds while he slid the palm of his other hand over the curves of the animal's body. He fed it an apple, then sat on a stool and picked up his rasp, not taking his attention off the horse until he was done. The horses stood stoically, their tails swishing back and forth. He cleaned gravel out of their hooves, trimmed the edges, and pounded nails through the holes in the new shoes.

When he finished the three horses, Dad wiped his hands on his jeans, broke the apple he had left in half, and passed me one of the halves. A tiny thrill zinged through me. None of my friends had fathers with hands strong enough to break an apple in half. But then none of my friends had fathers like mine.

Any time Dad went to a cattle auction in Vancouver, Mom's face stayed pinched all day. She twisted the skirt of her apron and paced. Sometimes she got one of her migraine headaches. We kids stayed quiet and listened as she said, again and again, "Your father can't be trusted. He loses sight of everything around animals." We all knew what Mom was afraid of. She had sent a list with Dad of the things we needed. A horse was never on it.

I went to one auction in Vancouver with Dad, in a low red barn with a dirt floor, reeking of sweaty, panicked animals and manure. I followed behind Dad with my hand over my mouth, holding my breath as the dirt and dust stirred up by the pawing cattle burned my nose. Crowded together in pens, the cattle bashed themselves against the rails and made pitiful, mooing sounds. Horses were kept in separate stalls, one for each. The stallions made all the noise. Unpredictable and dangerous, they whinnied screams of terror and slammed their powerful bodies against the boards of their stalls. My body trembled with fear while my heart jumped with excitement.

Men milled around inspecting the steers and heifers and talking to the owners of the horses. I stuck close to Dad, in his jeans and cowboy hat, weaving in and out among the small groups, and didn't let him out of my sight. He lingered around the horses' stalls and glanced at the milk cows.

Calves were sold first, led one by one to a platform with a table beside it, at the end of the barn. An auctioneer called out in a sing-song voice to people clustered in front, "Twenty-five-dollar bid, now twenty-six, now twenty-six, who'll give me twenty-six . . ." When no more hands went up, he hollered, "Going once, going twice, sold!" and slammed his wooden hammer on the table.

Dad moved in close when the cows were led to the platform. He waited while the first few were auctioned off, and then he waved at the auctioneer and bought a milk cow. "She's a Jersey," he said, pointing out her tan-and-white markings. "She'll give us lots of good cream." We drove up to the little house in the pickup after dark, with the cow securely tied to the raised sideboards in the back. Mom's body in the light of the open door eased in a grateful sigh.

The winter when I was four, I went with Dad to hunt down horses he had put out to pasture in Upper Gibsons. Before we left home, he slid on his work gloves and threw a couple of hay bales into the box of the pickup. He parked the Chev in an empty field off an isolated road. A rusted, barbed-wire fence lay on the ground beside the driveway. The grass was frozen flat. "I won't be long. I'll be back as soon as I rustle up those horses. They can't be far. You stay here and wait."

After a while I started to shiver. Snowflakes began to fall. Would Dad be gone for hours? The light inside the cab dimmed to dark and my cheeks went numb. Panic choked off my breath. What if I froze to death? Heart pounding, more frightened of dying than I was of Dad, I pushed open the door. Outside, everything was white: the sky, the field, the trees. Dad was nowhere in sight. The only sound was silence. "Dad. Dad. Are you there? Dad?" My voice came crashing back. I called again and again till I was hoarse. Dad didn't answer. *Please, God, don't let me freeze to death. I don't care how wonderful heaven is, I don't want to go there.*

I stumbled through the falling snow in the direction of Lower Gibsons and home. My feet lost all feeling. The faint lights of a log cabin came into view. I stood on the road outside, fear crushing my chest. Finally, I willed myself to inch forward and fell against the door with a bumping sound.

An older couple, stooped with age, and their adult daughter welcomed me in. The lights, the warmth of the cabin, and their kindness enveloped me with the comfort of a goose-feather eiderdown. The daughter sat me next to their blazing fireplace, made me a mug of cocoa, and gave me a piece of white bread with peanut butter and honey. My shivering eased. Was Dad going to be mad at me?

The gray-haired mother patted me on the shoulder as I hiccuped and sobbed. "Don't you worry, honey. Your father will search for you when he doesn't find you in the truck." Her husband hovered beside her and let her do the talking. "He's sure to knock on our door any minute now." When he did, my heart leapt.

"I thought she might be here," Dad said after the daughter opened the door to his snow-covered figure. He clunked his boots together and knocked the snow off before stepping inside onto their mat. "I was sure worried when I got back from feeding the horses and she wasn't in the truck." I sensed he was relieved to find me although embarrassed at the same time. What kind of parent leaves a four-year-old in a pickup during a snow storm? He didn't get mad at me for getting out.

On the drive home, Dad glanced over at me. "I think it's better if we don't tell your mother about this." He'd left me in the cold and people had found out about it. He'd probably forgotten he even had me with him until he got back to the truck. If I had gone to sleep as I'd done other times, would I have frozen to death?

The moment I decided to open the door of the cab and get out was a defining moment in my life. I had disobeyed Dad and acted to take care of myself. I was the only person I could count on, there was no one else. Mom wanted me out of the way. And I couldn't trust Dad to even remember he had me with him. I was sure that if Janice had gone with Dad instead of me, he would never have left her in the truck in below-zero weather.

He's My Brother

GIBSONS HAD NO HOSPITAL, only Dr. Inglis. Mom was going to stay with church members in Vancouver, near St. Paul's Hospital, while she waited for the baby. She leaned over her belly and kissed Rob, Sarah, Janice, and me goodbye. The ferry from Vancouver had just docked. Cars revved their engines and drove off the car deck, passing us where we waited on the government wharf.

Mom reached out and touched Sarah on the arm. "Now remember, be extra careful when you're cooking on the camp stove." At ten years old, Sarah was in charge of the house and the family: taking care of us kids, cooking the meals, and making Dad's lunches. She was staying off school while Mom was gone. When Rob got home on the school bus, he was supposed to help her. Dad would be at Mr. Pope's sawmill until after dark. "And you two," Mom focused on Janice and me, "no arguing or fighting. Listen to what Rob and Sarah tell you."

Dad pulled his handkerchief out of his jeans pocket, blew his nose, and then gave Mom a quick kiss on the cheek. "Telephone just as soon as you have the baby."

Mom lumbered onto the ferry carrying her small suitcase. She stopped at the bottom of the steps up to the passenger lounge, turned, studied us all, and then grasped the handrail. We waited until the ferry had pulled away from the dock and then climbed into the pickup. Everyone was quiet. I wished Mom was still with us until I remembered that as soon as we got home we were going to start on the surprise. It had taken everything in me not to blurt it out to her. Aunt Winnifred, Uncle Ted, and my cousins Nonie and Jennifer had moved to Vancouver Island. The proper house was empty. We were moving in.

As soon as we got home, we stuffed clothes, blankets, and kitchen dishes into cardboard boxes. Dad and Rob carted them over to the big house with our beds, the table and chairs, and the chesterfield. Neighbors helped Dad and Rob move the piano into our new living room.

We called our new home "the big house around the bay." It had a refrigerator in the kitchen, instead of the ice box we were used to, and a wood cookstove. There was even linoleum. We wouldn't be able to sweep dirt through holes in the floor as we had in the tool shed. And at last we had a real bathroom with a bathtub.

Dad and Rob set up Mom and Dad's bed in the living room. The baby would sleep beside them on top of their dresser, in one of the drawers. Dad surveyed the living room, cramped now with the bed, dresser, Mom's piano, and the chesterfield. He shook his head. "I'm going to have to build us another bedroom."

Rob's bed was set up in the small bedroom off the kitchen. Sarah, Janice, and I had the larger bedroom at the back of the house. Sarah had one of the bunk beds, and Janice and I shared the double bed that Aunt Winnifred and Uncle Ted had left behind.

That first night, I longed to be back in the little house. A stack of empty boxes was piled up on one side of the back bedroom. At bedtime Sarah found a quilt for the bottom of the box I had decided I wanted to sleep in. Rob held the sides and helped me climb in. In the morning I was cold and my muscles were sore. The second night I slept in the bed with Janice.

Each morning, Sarah cooked porridge for breakfast and made tomato sandwiches for lunch. Mom had baked two batches of bread and left us store-bought tomatoes. With summer over, the tomatoes from our garden were gone. Store-bought tomatoes were a luxury we had never had. They came in an oblong box with a celluloid lid. I watched one morning as Sarah, an apron tied around her waist, bent over the cutting board on the counter and carefully cut one of the tomatoes into as many slices as she could.

The days dragged. One night after supper, the telephone on

the kitchen wall rang. My breath stalled as Dad picked up the receiver. "It's a boy! A boy! Imagine that." After he hung up, he laughed and took turns dancing Janice and me around on his feet. "It's a boy, it's a boy," he sang. When he grabbed me to dance, I held onto him tight, my arms around his waist, my bare feet on top of his wool socks as he twirled me in dizzying circles.

A week later, Dad left the pickup parked on the wharf and we all walked onto the ferry. While we waited in Horseshoe Bay for Mom to be dropped off, Dad bought each of us kids a green bottle of orange crush and a foil bag of potato chips to share. The bottle was smooth and cool in my hands and the carbonated bubbles fizzed in my nose. It was my first taste of soda.

As soon as Mom arrived, she bent down and pulled back the blankets of the bundle in her arms to reveal the soft, sleeping face of my new brother. I had so many questions. I knew in a general way how babies were born, because Christine had told me they came out of the top of their mother's thighs. I puzzled over that, too embarrassed to reveal my ignorance and ask her how each of the legs split open.

What I was burning to know was what a spirit looked like and how and when my brother's spirit joined up with his body. In one of her Sunday school lessons, Mom had explained that it was important for families to have as many children as they could. "There are so many spirits waiting in heaven to come to earth and prove themselves worthy to return to God. The more children a family has, the more blessed that family is." No matter how many times I asked, she could never tell me what spirits looked like and how they joined up with a body.

Equally confusing was exactly how our family was blessed by having so many kids. While there was excitement over my baby brother's birth, children in our family were a burden rather than a blessing. Mom and Dad couldn't feed us all. Brent and Christine's families, who weren't Mormon, were entirely different. Christine had one sister and no brothers, and Brent had two brothers. They went to Sunday school at the United Church, had lots to eat, and wore clothes that fit them, and their parents took them on holidays each year to places like Disneyland in California. Christine even had her own wallet with money in it. The only holidays our family went on while I was growing up were two camping trips to Alberta and one to Salt Lake City.

Dad drove us home from the ferry with Mom and my new brother and turned into the driveway of the big house instead of the little house. As he did, Mom said, "Oh my, oh my." I wondered whether she was really surprised or was just pretending. Mom and Dad named my new brother Michael. By the time he was three months old, Mom was pregnant again, this time with Ian.

Ian was born two months ahead of time at Mrs. Jenkins's house. She was a retired nurse who lived across from Armour's Beach in Lower Gibsons. Dr. Inglis delivered him and he weighed four pounds. I had no idea how long a pregnancy was. All I knew was that when Ian was born, it wasn't the same as when Michael was born. One morning when I woke up, Mom wasn't in the kitchen. Sarah was stirring a pot of porridge on the stove. She yawned. "Mom had the baby last night at Nurse Jenkins's house. She woke me up before she left. Dad says it's another boy."

Why hadn't Mom gone into Vancouver to the hospital? Dad wasn't dancing around and laughing, the way he had when Mom phoned about Michael. I knew better than to ask any questions. Dad, Rob, and Sarah were quiet as we ate breakfast. Janice and I kept quiet too. Sarah changed Michael's diapers and dressed him. Even he didn't make his usual noise when she fed him rice cereal in his high chair.

After breakfast, Dad glanced over at Janice and me. "If you behave yourselves, you can visit Mom with Rob and Sarah." Relief surged through me. Mom must be okay. Before we left, Sarah said to me, "Wash your hands and face and for goodness sake don't you dare blow your nose on the sleeve of your coat while we're there."

We trooped up the steep flight of steps to the back door of the nurse's house. I grinned with anticipation. Dad, carrying Michael in his arms, had on the fedora he wore when we went to church in

Vancouver. A plump woman with rosy cheeks, wearing a spider-web hairnet, led us into a dim hallway toward a half-closed door.

Mom sat upright, supported by pillows, in a bed that filled the room. A lamp cast shadows around her head and onto the bed jacket she wore. Dark circles rimmed her eyes. In her arms was a bundle of blankets. Although the room was warm, she never unwrapped the bundle. I couldn't breathe. I thought Mom would be happy. My eyes never left her face while she talked to Dad. Neither of them smiled. We were only allowed to stay a few minutes.

That afternoon, Dad drove Mom and the baby into Vancouver to St. Paul's Hospital. Sarah would have to stay off school again while Mom was away. Dad came home on the last ferry, slumped onto a kitchen chair, and closed his eyes. I tiptoed to my bedroom.

A week later he picked up Mom from the ferry. At suppertime, we heard the truck pull into the driveway and the doors bang shut. Rob, Sarah, Janice, and I rushed out to meet her. Michael watched through the bars of his playpen. Mom's face was pale. "The baby will have to stay in an incubator for a month." Her voice was somber. "Dad and I have decided to call him Ian. He's started to gain weight, but I'm worried that he'll lose his sight from the oxygen he needs to help his lungs develop."

That night I knelt beside my bed. *Please, God, don't let the baby go blind.* The only blind person I had ever seen was a lady at my grandma's house where Mom grew up. The summer after Michael was born, Dad had driven us to southern Alberta. Grandma invited the blind woman for dinner after Sunday school. She dished up the woman's food and told her, as if it was the face of a clock, which part of the plate the vegetables, mashed potatoes, and roast beef were on.

I was the only one at home during the day to help Mom with Michael after Rob, Sarah, and Janice took the bus to school. That first morning that we were on our own, Mom stayed in her bed in the living room and pulled the covers close around her. "Will you get me a cold cloth for my head? I've got another one of my headaches."

I was used to helping Mom when she had a migraine. I pretended I was a nurse, running a washcloth under the cold water tap in the bathroom, wringing it out, and gently laying it over her eyes. When I was sure she was asleep, I inched a chair over to the refrigerator, climbed onto it, and reached up to turn the radio on. My heart pounded. I wasn't supposed to touch the radio, but I wanted to listen to the kindergarten program Mom usually turned on for me. I glanced over at her. She didn't stir. I turned the dial till it clicked. The man's voice was barely audible. Michael played on the floor beside me. Mom didn't wake up.

In the afternoon, I sat beside her bed while she talked about Tommy. He was born while Rob and Sarah were both in diapers. "We were on the farm just outside of town, when Tommy got sick." Her voice quivered. I stayed absolutely still. "I wanted to take him to the doctor. He was having trouble breathing. We didn't have a telephone, electricity, or even running water. Your father insisted that there was nothing to worry about, that he would give Tommy a blessing."

Dad held the highest and the most powerful priesthood in the church. He had rubbed a drop of mineral oil, sanctified by prayer and called consecrated oil, on Tommy's head, cradled his head in his hands, and said a prayer of healing.

"Tommy got sicker." Mom sat up straighter in bed, shifted the pillows behind her back, and cleared her throat. I twisted my hands in my lap. "Our Dodge truck was broken down and there was snow on the ground. All we had was a team of horses and a wagon we used to go to church in. I finally persuaded your father to ask one of our neighbors for a ride to the hospital, about twenty miles away."

She had told me the story before. Part of me wanted to hear the ending and another part of me didn't. "The neighbor smoked while he was driving. I'm sure that made it even harder for Tommy to breathe. When we got to the hospital, I handed his frail body into the arms of a nurse. He died a half an hour later." Her eyes misted over.

My breath stuck in my chest. I moved to the end of the bed and gripped the rail. Mom blamed Dad for Tommy's death. According to the church, Dad was ordained by God as the head of the house and the final authority on all decisions. Mom believed she had no choice but to do what he wanted whether she agreed or not. I didn't understand then that this was one of the reasons she railed against Dad's bad decisions while remaining firmly entrenched in martyrdom. Mom was smarter than Dad. Better educated, she carefully thought situations through ahead of time and didn't break whatever was at hand when she was angry, as Dad did. The church had given Dad authority over Mom and she went along with it. She wasn't smart about that part. Would Tommy be alive if Dad had taken him to the doctor when Mom first asked? The blessing Dad had given Tommy hadn't made him better. There had to be something faulty with the priesthood and Dad's belief in its power.

A piece of Mom's heart was back in Alberta buried in a shallow winter grave marked with a wooden cross. Dad hadn't listened to Mom or acted on her instinct as a mother. She hadn't trusted or acted on it herself. Was Mom fixated on Tommy's death because she was afraid Ian would die too? She dabbed at her eyes with the bed sheet. "He's in heaven waiting for us to join him." Goosebumps pricked my arms. Was he watching us?

Ian lived. When he came out of the incubator, he had his sight although he was delicate and quiet. Something had happened to Mom, though. Part of her was gone. I didn't know then that her disappearance was called postpartum depression. Even if she had been aware that there was something wrong with how she thought and felt, she would never have sought help from Dr. Inglis. He gave shots of penicillin accompanied by Scotch mints. Mom's belief that she needed to have as many children as she could to get into heaven, while being submissive to Dad, couldn't be cured by any medicine. If she wanted to be a queen in heaven, this was the price she had to pay.

All Mom had ahead of her were more pregnancies, more children than she could take care of, and more poverty. She was married for eternity to Dad, who didn't listen to her and who did what he wanted, when he wanted. What woman wouldn't be depressed?

On a Roll

WHY DID SHE DO IT? At the time, I didn't even think that question. I was wrapped up in Mom's world, without a world of my own, and had no reference for anything else. Only as an adult, from the safety of independence, did the horror of what she had done or tried to do surface. Did she plan and act deliberately? Or was she simply neglectful, with her judgment impaired by depression?

What mother who loved her children would be so careless with them? And why us girls instead of the boys? In the context of the church, the second question answered itself. All that is certain is that when she did it, Mom was beyond rational thought and behavior, inside a bubble where nothing made sense. As a child, I was in the bubble with her. It was all I knew.

That June morning she sighed as she plunked Michael, child number five, into the kitchen sink for a bath. "Four children is all I have the energy for," she told me. Ian, child number six, was asleep in his crib. Her body sagged as if she could barely stand. She pushed the water faucet out of the way, picked up a washcloth, and bent over Michael. He laughed and splashed in the sink with dimpled hands. Water sprayed onto Mom's apron all the way through to her housedress. "Oooh!" She jumped back. "Stop that! Right now! I mean it!" Michael started to wail. She dumped him onto a towel on the counter and roughly dried him with another. His skin went all red and he shrieked louder. Her eyes closed and tears rolled down her face. She would have to change her clothes.

The week before, she had been happy. The whole family had taken the ferry into Vancouver for a church conference. At the all-day meetings, the stake president, head of all the congregations in the Vancouver area, read sermons from the church presidency in Salt Lake City. As Mom sat or stood beside Dad, handsome in his suit, each of them holding one of the boys, she smiled with her whole being.

Back at home, she hung up her coat and drooped. It was hard for me to remember what Mom had been like before Ian was born. She looked the same, but she was different. "I don't care if it's still light outside," she yelled at Janice and me from the kitchen each night. "Get back into bed and stay there." I couldn't see her but I was sure there was a grimace on her face. She never read us bedtime stories anymore. I missed the mother who had. Each night that spring and summer after Ian came home, I lay in bed with the sheets pushed to one side and listened to the laughter of my friends on the street outside. Before Ian, Mom let Janice and me play outside with our friends until dark.

The morning that she did it, after she dressed Michael and changed out of her wet dress, Mom asked Janice and me, "Do you two want to come for a ride? I've got to get nails for Dad. I don't want you under his feet slowing him down." Dad and Rob were building another bedroom onto the back of the house. "Sarah can take care of Michael and Ian while we're away." I didn't suspect a thing.

The drive into Lower Gibsons took about five minutes. I sat next to Mom. I didn't care that Janice got the window seat. She always hogged it, it wasn't worth a fight. We passed the water pumps for the village, the drug store, and the gas station. Mom turned toward the ocean just before Dr. Inglis's house. She parked the truck in front of the United Church across from Knowles Hardware. The nose of the Chev pointed to the steep ramp of the government wharf and the ocean below.

As Mom got out of the pickup, she said, "The emergency brake doesn't work. If the truck starts to roll, just press on the brake pedal right there." She pointed to a row of black rubber pieces under the steering wheel. "I'll be right back." The door slammed shut with a bang. She was gone before I could ask her which of the pedals she meant. Janice hadn't paid any attention.

I watched Mom tuck her purse under her arm, pat down her hair, and dash across the street. The skirt of her cotton dress flared out around her legs. As the door of the hardware store closed behind her, the pickup started to roll. My stomach flipped over.

I pressed hard with my foot on one of the black pedals. The truck didn't stop. Vomit rose. I stamped on all of the pedals. "It doesn't work!" I shrieked to Janice. "It doesn't work!" She crashed into me and pounded the pedals with her feet. The truck kept rolling. We screamed. The truck gathered speed. We thrashed against each other, howling and smashing at the pedals. The truck kept rolling.

Suddenly, the door on the driver's side was yanked open. A man shoved us out of the way, leapt onto the seat, and slammed the pedals to the floor. The truck stopped.

The stranger, and Janice and I, sat in the pickup with the door hanging open in the middle of the road at the top of the ramp. Janice and I cried and shook. When my eyes finally focused, I noticed that the man's hands on the steering wheel were big and strong. A worker's hands. He wore a plaid shirt and jeans and work boots, and smelled of sweat and cigarette smoke. I loved his smell. I wanted to collapse onto him, cling to him, and moan thank you, thank you. Thank you for saving us.

"Whe-ew," he finally breathed out, pushing the pedals on the floor and shifting the gear stick. "It's in reverse now. You're safe. This sucker's not gonna budge an inch. You're two lucky little girls." Mom came out of the hardware store then, with a paper bag in her hand. Her eyes narrowed and her mouth tightened.

"Just what do you think you're doing in my pickup?" Her voice was nasty. I didn't understand. Her face twisted with anger. Why wasn't she throwing her arms around the man and thanking him for saving us from drowning?

"What the hell does it look like, lady?" he roared and got out. His face was red, the same as Dad's when he got mad. A vein throbbed in his neck. "You just about lost your kids. Your truck was headed for the wharf. It wasn't even in gear. You're not fit to be a mother. You're lucky you didn't lose the kids and the truck. She's all yours!" He stomped away.

For a moment, Mom stood beside the truck with her mouth open, her face white. She climbed in, banged the door, revved the engine, and tore through the village. "What a lot of silliness," she said as the pickup rounded a curve in the road. "I told you girls to push the brake in if the truck started to move."

"Mom," I croaked, "we did. We pushed all the pedals really hard and the truck wouldn't stop. I thought we were going to die, I was so scared." I shivered and cried. Janice made hoarse, gasping noises.

"Well, you didn't and you're still here." Mom turned hard into our driveway. The wheels of the pickup spat gravel as she slammed on the brakes and wrenched off the engine. She leapt out of the truck and marched to the back of the house. Janice and I crept after her. "Clarence!" she shrieked, her hands on her hips. "How many times have I asked you to fix that emergency brake?" Dad was bent over, halfway through sawing a piece of two-by-four laid across saw horses. His head came up. Mom's face was red and her eyes bulged. "The truck started to roll on the hill when I parked it," she shrieked. "A stranger jumped in and stopped it. I was so embarrassed. You don't care, do you? You just don't care." Her voice ended in a squeak.

"Well, why did you park it on a hill anyway?" Dad hollered back. "Didn't you put it in reverse before you got out? Or put a rock under one of the wheels? How stupid is that? It's your own darn fault. Did you get the nails?" Mom whirled away, around the side of the house and into the kitchen. She sat on a chair, laid her face on the table, and cried. Wrenching sobs tore out of her. She'd left the bag of nails on the floor of the pickup. Janice and I tiptoed past. Sarah stood beside the sink, eyes wide, mouth open.

My body stayed jittery all day. I was still in the truck rolling to the water. In the nights that followed, I dreamed I was above the truck yet inside as it flew through the air. Icy water closed over me. As everything went black I jolted awake, gasping to breathe, my heart pounding so hard my chest hurt.

I searched the streets for the man who leapt into the truck. I wanted to thank him and tell him how sorry I was that Mom got mad at him and that I would love him forever for saving me and my sister Janice. Months later, I was still scanning men's faces. I never set eyes on him again. When I finally stopped searching, I was more alone than ever.

Missionaries

ONCE A MONTH on a Saturday morning, Dad and Rob drove to the government dock to meet the ferry. Dad searched for two clean-shaven young men with short hair, dressed in suits, and carrying briefcases. The missionaries were easy to spot in the crowd of loggers and mill workers who streamed off the boat.

At home, Janice and I put the boys' toys and clothes away and made sure all the beds were made. Sarah swept the floors and scrubbed the linoleum. The aromas of the special meals Mom always made for the visiting missionaries wafted through the house: a pot of homemade soup bubbling on the stove and loaves of bread cooling on the kitchen counter. If Mom didn't have money to buy groceries for this monthly feast, the store halfway up the hill let her take home what she needed. She paid for the food we'd already eaten out of Dad's next paycheck.

The chug of the pickup on the road was my signal to shout, "They're here." Mom quickly changed into a clean apron. The young men were Mormon missionaries, called "elders," the designation of priesthood they held in the church hierarchy. Usually just out of high school, they weren't much older than Rob. They had committed two years of their lives to finding new members for the church, living all the while off their savings and donations from their families and home congregations.

The church in Salt Lake City had a mission headquarters in Vancouver. Different young men were sent from the mission home each month. They traveled throughout the province and never stayed in one place for any length of time. They could be from anywhere in the world, although they all spoke English. Most

47

were teenagers. According to church rules, we weren't allowed to call them by their first names. Instead, we called them Elder with their last name.

On a Saturday morning in the summer, when Dad and Rob arrived home with the missionaries, they were all laughing. "This is Elder Christmas," Dad said to Mom, as if it was one of his jokes. "And Elder Swanson." Both missionaries wore gray suits and had crew cuts.

"Elder Christmas?" Mom raised her eyebrows.

"Yes," Dad laughed. "I thought he was having me on when we picked them up. So I told him my name was Father New Year's. Ha, ha, ha."

While we waited to eat lunch, the elders answered our questions about their families and where they lived. I was fascinated with Elder Swanson's description of his home in California, with oranges hanging from trees in his back yard. I might get half an orange once or twice a year.

Before they sat down to lunch, they took off their suit jackets and draped them over their chairs. Even though the doors and all the windows were open, it was still so hot that perspiration glistened on their faces and formed semicircles in the underarms of their white, short-sleeved shirts. "It's hot enough out there to fry an egg on the road," Dad said after giving a blessing on the food. "On my mission we took off our jackets and carried them. We couldn't have stood it otherwise. In Texas, it's the humidity that gets to a fella."

"There's nothing I'd like better than to take my jacket off when we knock on doors today," Elder Swanson said. "It's against church rules." That was just one of the rules that didn't make any sense to me.

"Maybe just this one time," Elder Christmas said slowly. He'd been on his mission the longest and made the decisions for both of them. "It's not as if there's anyone here who's going to report us to the mission home in Vancouver." If someone had, how would the church have punished them?

After lunch, I walked with them to the end of our driveway and watched them amble down the road carrying their briefcases. Waves of heat shimmered off the asphalt. The grass on either side of the road was brown and dry. They didn't bother knocking on our neighbors' doors: earlier missionaries had been turned away. Although our neighbors weren't interested in learning about the church, they kept a close eye on what Mom and Dad did and how we kids behaved.

"The rule about having to wear their jackets even in this heat doesn't make sense," I said to Mom back in the kitchen.

"It's the image that's important." She was feeding Ian rice cereal in his highchair. She paused, a spoonful hovering midair between the bowl and his mucky-lipped mouth. "How they present themselves to the world when they represent the church is what matters."

That night for supper we had bread with milk and sugar, which neither of these missionaries had had before. I was thankful to an elder who once told us that his family sprinkled sugar on their bread. After that, our sugar bowl always came to the table.

Elder Christmas was a concert pianist, and after supper he sat down at Mom's piano. His fingers rippled over the keys. The music rose and fell, swelling through the house and spilling out the open doors and windows. Shivers ran through me and the skin on my arms rose in goosebumps. None of the neighbors complained. The following week, some of them told Mom and Dad that they had enjoyed the music.

We sang "Nearer My God to Thee," "How Firm a Foundation," and "Praise to the Man." My whole being vibrated. When I went to bed that night, my body was weightless, as if I was floating.

The missionaries slept on the floor in Rob's room on beds made of quilts. In the morning, I wondered whether their muscles ached as mine had the time I slept in the cardboard box. If they did, neither of them mentioned it. After breakfast, Elder Christmas played the piano for Sunday school in the living room. Both of the elders talked about how much they loved the church. "I know that Joseph Smith was a true prophet of God," Elder Swanson said as he stood beside the piano and bore his testimony. "And that the Church of Jesus Christ of Latter-day Saints is the true church here on earth."

They served us the sacrament, something Dad did when we were on our own for home Sunday school. The sacrament was bread broken into pieces, served on a silver candy dish, and water in whisky shot glasses that had been prayed over. It was to remember that Jesus Christ had died on the cross and to remind members of the promises they had made when they were baptized. I had yet to be baptized but I was still served the sacrament. I rolled the tiny piece of bread around on my tongue to make it last, even though it was the same bread we had every day.

After Sunday school, Sarah helped Mom fry chicken she had taken from the freezer the night before. Dad jostled Michael and Ian on his legs while he and Rob talked to the elders in the living room. Mom put the extra leaves in our round oak table, spread a white linen cloth over top, and handed down the silverware box from the top of the piano to Janice and me. Mom's parents had given her and Dad the twelve-piece setting of silver for a wedding present. The floured pieces of chicken sizzled to a crisp golden brown and tantalizing aromas floated throughout the house. My mouth watered in anticipation of the wing I would get.

At Sunday dinner, Dad asked Elder Christmas and Elder Swanson what their plans were when they finished their missions. "We're exempted from the military draft by going on a mission," Elder Swanson said. He rested his fork on his plate while he talked. "When I get back home, I'm going straight to college. I can get a further draft exemption if I do."

Elder Christmas laughed. "By the time he finishes college, if he finds a wife and starts a family within a year he'll be able to avoid the draft altogether. That's what most of us try to do. My girl is waiting at home for me."

Mom stopped eating and buttered the bun on her side plate. "Why should our young men serve in the military when they don't have to? I think war is a terrible thing. Scripture says we should be part of the world but not of it."

Dad drove Elder Christmas and Elder Swanson to the afternoon ferry. I regretted the end of their visit and with it the end of the stories and happiness they brought with them. Both Mom and Dad smiled and laughed while they were with us, even though the only thing they had in common with the missionaries was their belief in the church. In all the years the missionaries knocked on doors in Gibsons, they never found anyone other than Mom and Dad who wanted to talk about Mormonism.

The Sawmill

WHEN MR. POPE PUSHED DAD to work on Sundays, Dad quit and started up his own operation, a sawmill on the road to Port Mellon. According to the church, the Sabbath belonged to the Lord and Sundays were for worship.

It was now up to Dad to ensure that there was a steady supply of logs to feed the saws at his mill. He sourced out timber from logging camps up and down the Sunshine Coast. In the first few months, after supper Dad drank water with baking soda in it to settle his stomach. I watched him grimace as he gulped it down in one go.

Mom did the books. She took the checks that came in the mail to the bank and paid all the bills. Whatever was left after she paid the church and the expenses for the mill was for our family. She worked at the kitchen table with a heavy, green adding machine, a ledger book, and a stack of invoices.

"You're my best little helper," Mom told me every morning after Rob, Sarah, and Janice left for the school bus. I was eager to start school with them the following September. If it wasn't raining when Mom did the books, I took the boys outside to play. I pushed Ian around in an old buggy one of the neighbors had given Mom and let Michael stand on the footstep. I parked the buggy with Ian in it by the side of the road, waited for a car to appear at the corner, and raced with Michael in front of the car to the other side of the road.

One weekday afternoon when Dad was away at a logging camp in Sechelt, an hour's drive up the coast, a man walked into the middle of our driveway. I noticed him from the kitchen window.

He stood completely still and waited. A shiver shuddered through me. "Mom," I called, my body pulsing with a scared kind of excitement. "There's a tramp, a real tramp, standing in our driveway."

She paused at the window, her eyes on the man, then walked outside. I followed and stood beside her, my jaw tight, my feet rooted to the dirt. A dusty hat, a fedora identical to the one Dad wore to church in Vancouver, perched on his head. He had on an old suit jacket that was way too big for him and baggy pants, and he smelled of cigarette smoke. "I need pay," he said in broken English. "For work I do." His eyes were red-rimmed and watery. I moved a step back.

"I'm so sorry, I don't have any money for you today." Mom held her hands open. I flushed with embarrassment for her. The man twisted his hat in his hands. I wanted him to leave. He was the only one of the sawmill crew who had ever come to the house.

"Our family doesn't have any money either." Mom squinted into the sun. "If I had it I'd give it to you. I'm waiting for some lumber payments to come in. As soon as they do, you'll have your paycheck." The man stayed silent. My eyes darted from him to Mom, then back to him. He didn't move. Mom held up her hand. "Just wait a minute." She walked into the house. I followed and stopped at the bottom of the steps, ready to bolt inside if the man moved.

Mom came outside with a warm loaf of bread she had just baked, wrapped in a piece of newspaper. The man's eyes stayed empty. His mouth closed in a tight line. He put his fedora back on his head, took the loaf of bread Mom held out, and without a word turned and walked out of the driveway. I hoped that he wouldn't ever come back.

After breakfast the next morning, while I washed the dishes, Mom started in on Dad. "Clarence, if the McManns paid us what they owe, that would take care of everything for at least a few months. What did Mr. McMann say when you told him how much he owed us?"

"I hate to push the old man because he always pays up. Why

don't you just type up a nice reminder letter with the amounts?" My eyes went from Mom to Dad. I knew that Dad hadn't asked for the money. He procrastinated when it came to collecting what he was owed. I always thought it was because he wanted everyone to like him and think of him as a good guy, until it occurred to me that he was unsure of himself and anxious about standing up for himself. He depended on Mom to ask people for money.

"No." Mom planted her hands on her hips and glowered at him. "You promised to talk to him. You keep putting it off. We need the money now. The men need to be paid. I've had enough of it!" She threw up her hands. "Oh! You can be so exasperating!" She slammed out the kitchen door with the laundry basket under her arm and the clothes-peg bag in her hand. Dad would talk to Mr. McMann for sure. Mom would cry all day and ignore him until he did.

One spring morning, after I had asked Dad countless times to go to the sawmill, he took me with him. "I'm only going for a while today. If you come with me, you've got to stay close and not wander." Dad sat on the back steps and laced up his steel-toed boots. He grabbed his hard hat and jammed work gloves into the back pocket of his jeans.

The sawmill was a collection of greasy machines with pulleys and claws dangling from a high roof. There were no walls. Conveyer belts and dangerous saws screamed. I jumped every time one of them started up. Dad didn't have to remind me to stick close. A truck piled high with logs shook the ground as it roared up the driveway. Pine, fir, and cedar oozing sap were stacked in piles in the yard.

Dad's crew of six were unshaven men in dirty clothes and steel-toed boots, covered in sawdust and smelling of the outdoors and sweat. Their raucous voices and joking laughter shocked me, and I was sure none of them went to any church. They used swear words, even "God Dam," and got drunk as soon as they finished work.

Dad complained to Mom one night as they sat at the table after supper. "You'd think that Dave would have more sense. I had to send him home again today to sober up."

"What he needs is the gospel." Mom drew invisible patterns on the table with a clean knife. She had taught us in one of her Sunday school lessons that drinking beer or whiskey—in the clear, flat bottles that men pulled from their back trouser pockets—was wrong. It was against church rules. When I found an empty whiskey bottle by the side of the road one afternoon, I sniffed at it and the fumes burned up my nose. Whiskey had a bitter, rotten kind of stench. How could anyone want to swallow it?

Dad dragged himself through the back door each day after he finished work. He set his battered lunch kit and hard hat on the kitchen counter and groaned as he bent over to unlace his boots. Every time I saw how tired he was, I wished he didn't have to stay so late at the mill. If he didn't have all of us kids, I thought, he wouldn't have to work so hard.

After he took off his boots, he slumped in a chair next to the woodstove and put his feet up on the open oven door. He usually asked Janice and me, "Will you rub my feet? They hurt like the dickens." We took turns, our small fingers stumbling over the mended bits on the heels of his socks. When we rubbed his feet, his eyes closed and soft snoring sounds issued from his nose and throat. We giggled and whispered, "He's gone to sleep."

One day when I was five, Dad came home in the middle of the afternoon. The logs had run out. The shipment he had been promised was two days late and he'd had to shut the mill down. I noticed when he came in the kitchen door that the air around him was tight, quivery, like an elastic band stretched to the limit.

Michael was in his high chair banging on the tray with a spoon. Mom was scrubbing carrots in the sink. Ian was asleep in his crib. Rob and Sarah were outside. Janice and I were running after each other between the kitchen and the living room. Dad snarled, "Marnie, can't you keep those darn kids quiet?" Startled, I paused, then kept after Janice.

"They're only children, Clarence, let them be." Mom rinsed the carrots under the tap.

Janice had promised that if I caught her, she would let me play with the blonde-haired doll she had gotten for Christmas. She had it in her hand. It was pretty and plump, with blue eyes and pink lips. My doll had black hair, a skinny body, and harsh red lips. I thought it was ugly. I tagged Janice and squealed, "Ha, ha, it's my turn to play with it now," and grabbed onto her doll.

"No, it's mine, you can't have it." I pulled harder. Janice wouldn't let go. "Mom," she screamed. "Mom, it's my doll, not hers."

Dad exploded. "Stop that! Stop that noise right now!" His chair went flying. From its hook on the wall, he grabbed the long wire toaster we used to toast bread on the stove. Janice and I froze. The doll clunked onto the floor.

"If you want to fight, I'll give you something to fight about! C'mon, *fight!*" His arm came down on us. The toaster slashed into my arm and pain shot up my shoulder. I screamed. Janice shrieked as it slashed her. The toaster came down again and again on our bare arms and legs, corralling us together. We howled. Dad sneered. "Hit her! Go on! Hit her!"

Paralyzed, I couldn't move, yet I was afraid not to try. All I could do was bump against Janice and flail stiff arms. I screamed and moaned. Janice cried. Dad laughed. Foam frothed from his mouth. Veins popped out in his neck. His spittle spattered all over me. He dropped the toaster and ripped off his belt. "Fight! You wanna fight? I'll teach you to fight!" His belt whistled through the air.

"Stop, Clarence! Stop! That's enough. Stop!" Mom's scream was far away.

Dad leapt and danced. His belt raised welts on my back, on my arms, on my legs. I keened and shrieked as the leather stung into me. I forgot about Janice. Thwack! Thwack! The thud of the belt and Dad's hysterical laughter thundered in my ears. He knocked me to the floor. I tried to crawl away. He grabbed me by the arm and yanked me up. "Get up and fight! I'll teach you to fight!" His voice was hoarse.

As suddenly as he began, he stopped. His body sagged and he staggered against the kitchen counter. The metal belt buckle clanked to the floor. He dragged the back of his hand across his mouth. I heard hoarse, wrenching sobs before realizing they were coming out of Janice and me. Mom came into focus. She had Michael, who was crying, on one hip. Ian screamed from his crib. "Clarence," she said. There was a stillness in her voice as she touched him on the arm. "Clarence, come outside." She opened the back door and he followed.

I crawled under the covers of my bed. My body burned and throbbed. I cried and shook. None of what had happened made any sense. Dad had become a madman and Mom hadn't been able to stop him. Eventually, the bruises and welts on my body healed, but something inside me stayed broken. Mom never said anything to me about what Dad had done, and Dad acted as if nothing had happened. I loved the dad who teased and was kind, the one who bought maple walnut ice cream in the summer, in round two-and-a-half gallon tubs, for us kids, and yard-long boxes of cones. I hated the stranger he'd become, the stranger who had hurt Janice and me. The other dad would never have hurt Janice. He might have gotten mad at me, but never at Janice. I was wary around this stranger, terrified he would erupt again without warning. When I stood next to him, I was afraid to get too close and kept a distance within myself. From then on, every part of me stayed tense and watchful.

Despair settled inside me and refused to leave. Just as the sawmill altered the logs, Dad's beating changed me forever. I never talked to anyone about what he had done. Even if I could have, there was no one to tell. The shame of it stayed locked inside me. Dad had reduced me to an animal willing to hurt my sister. When might he do it again? On the outside I acted the same and everyone thought I was happy. It was on the inside that I was different: I was afraid of everything.

As far as I was aware, Janice never talked about it either. She appeared to carry on as if nothing had happened. Yet when she was annoyed, her viciousness increased. She was always angry and talked to me in Dad's voice, nasty and sneering. Mom and Dad let her get away with it; they didn't even notice. The closeness between us was gone and never returned, although Janice stood up for me if anyone else tried to bully me. She wasn't afraid of anyone or anything. At school, she smashed a smaller boy over the head with her metal lunch kit. He needed stitches to close the gash she had laid open in his scalp. Mom let her stay home from school for a few days to let the horror of what she'd done subside.

My only reprieve was when I played with my friends Brent or Christine at their houses. I greedily absorbed their warmth and happiness. The lightness that came home with me hovered for a short while, then disappeared. The need to leave home grew. I squirreled away newspapers, wrapped my clothes in them, and hid the bundles under my side of the bed. I didn't want to alert anyone of my plan to run.

Each night I lay awake after Mom and Dad were asleep. Where could I go? The only place I could think of was the forest. Whenever Mom and Dad had one of their fights, the woods always took me in. How could I build a shelter that would keep me warm against the winter snow? And when the berries in the summer were gone, how would I feed myself?

I could think of no place to run to, and began instead to run away to places in my mind.

Mormon Underwear

MOM BOUGHT ME new underwear for my first year of school from the Simpsons-Sears catalog. She unwrapped the brown-paper parcel, held up a pair, and frowned. "Oh, these won't do at all. The legs are too loose. They'll gape wide open and all the boys at school will be able to see right up your underpants."

My face flushed. Had she found out I played doctor with Brent in the woods? Had Brent told? He couldn't have; he'd be in trouble along with me. Had someone seen us? I knew, without anything ever being said, that pulling down my pants with Brent was something I had to keep secret. I didn't want to stop. I got breathless and tingly when we played doctor.

Over the summer, I scanned the pages of children's clothes in the catalog so often that there were smudge marks on the pictures from my fingers. Mom had promised to buy me new shoes and the underwear for grade one. Pictured on the underwear page beside the plain white was a stack of delicate, lace-trimmed panties in pink, yellow, and blue. A smiling blonde girl, so perfect she could have been a doll, wore a pair of the pink panties and a matching lace undershirt.

"Mom, these are so-o beautiful." Faint with desire, I sat at the kitchen table one afternoon and pointed to the colors fanned out on the page. "Can we get these for school?" I was sure, even though I had brown hair, that they would make me look as elegant as the blonde girl in the catalog. I imagined the snap of the thin elastic around my legs and waist and the silky material sliding on my bare skin.

"We don't have money for frivolous things." Mom's voice was

sharp. She sat across from me mending one of Dad's gray work socks. "They won't last any time at all. They're made of flimsy material." I slumped in my chair and blinked back tears. I knew she'd probably say no, but I wanted them so much I hoped this one time she might say yes.

"When you get married, all you'll wear are white temple garments, not fancy colored underwear, so you may as well get used to it now." She finished the heel of Dad's sock, bit off the end of the thread, and picked up another. "Garments are sacred. They'll protect you from the evil in the world if you wear them day and night." She was talking about the baggy Mormon underwear she wore. Everyone in the family knew about the garments. We weren't supposed to talk about them—ever. If anyone outside the family asked us about the special underwear Mormons wore, we were not supposed to answer.

I had never seen Mom in her garments, only watched them fluttering on the clothesline. Neighbors noticed them. On washday, some of the women slowed down in front of our house and inspected our clothesline. I examined the garments on the line one morning, up close, when Mom wasn't around. Some of the pairs had to be Dad's. A picture of him wearing temple garments popped into my mind. I thought of something else right away.

Temple garments were made of thin, white material all in one piece, with short arms and legs. There were buttons down the front and special markings embroidered on the chest, at the waist, and above one of the knees. When the wind blew them straight out on the line, the part between the legs separated and opened up. That had to be so Mom could go to the bathroom without taking them off. I shuddered at the thought of how difficult it must be to pee without getting them all wet.

Mom's underwear was different than any of the pictures of ladies' underwear in the catalog Janice and I giggled over when no one was around. Mom didn't wear sleeveless dresses or blouses or short shorts in the summer. If she had, her sacred temple garments would have shown.

Mom folded Dad's mended socks together in a pair and gave me her full attention. "From the day you're married in the temple, you'll wear garments." I squirmed. The thought of being encased in clingy material made me feel sweaty and uncomfortable. "God wants women to be modest and keep their bodies covered." Mom's voice held a note of surety that brooked no argument.

One afternoon before Mom's birthday, Sarah, Janice, and I shopped for a present for her at a store in Lower Gibsons. Sarah told the saleslady how much money she had to spend, and the lady showed us a pair of dainty yellow panties. "Your mother will absolutely love these. Any woman would be thrilled to receive these as a gift." She smiled. Her teeth sparkled against her red lipstick.

I glanced at Sarah and Janice out of the corner of my eye. I knew in my heart they weren't the right kind of underwear for Mom because she only wore temple garment underwear, yet I didn't know how to tell the saleslady. Mom had told us never to talk about temple garments. I waited for Sarah and Janice to say that they wanted to look at something else, but they didn't say anything. Sarah paid for the panties with money she had earned from babysitting. The saleslady wrapped them in crumply layers of tissue paper, tucked them in a little brown bag, and handed it to Sarah. As we walked out of the shop, the bell on the door jangled loudly. I gulped. "Mom's not gonna be happy." I was sorry that Sarah had wasted her babysitting money and I was worried about what Mom would say.

"I couldn't tell the saleslady why Mom won't wear these." Sarah clutched the bag away from her. "We're not supposed to talk about anything to do with the temple. I couldn't think of any way to get out of buying them." My feet were heavy as we trudged home and we didn't talk much.

On Mom's birthday, after we ate supper and the cake Sarah had baked, Sarah gave her our present. Filled with dread I held my breath. I was sure Sarah and Janice did too. None of us moved. Mom folded back the tissue and stared down at the flimsy scrap of material. Her eyebrows furrowed. "Hmm." Her voice was low. The whole family stayed quiet. "You know I wear temple garments. What were you thinking?" The three of us kept our eyes on the table. Mom tucked the tissue over the panties and took them with her into the bedroom. I didn't see them again. We had let Mom down. Even though the panties were beautiful, they didn't fit into God's plan.

At the start of September, the night before my first day of grade one, Mom sewed elastic into the legs of my white cotton underpants. It was after supper and she had put Michael and Ian to bed. The back door was open in the late summer heat, but I was still hot and sticky. Standing in one spot while she measured the length of elastic around the top of each of my legs was hard to do. "Stop fidgeting and stand still." Mom gave my knee a pinch.

"Ouch."

"I want to get it right the first time." She sighed and nudged my leg. I carefully turned a couple of inches. The straight pins scratched if I moved faster than she could pin. I didn't want to make her more annoyed than she was.

The morning of my first day of school, I pulled on a pair of my new underwear, a white short-sleeved blouse, and the red plaid skirt with straps over the shoulders that Janice had worn the year before. At recess and lunch that day, I carefully kept my skirt down when we played outside. None of the boys had an opportunity to look up my skirt, let alone try and see past the snug bands that secured my underpants around the top of my legs.

On the second day of school, I forgot all about Mom's lecture on modesty and hung upside down by my knees from the top bar of the swings.

The House on the Hill

"MOM AND I JUST BOUGHT the Cartwright place overlooking the harbor." Dad sprawled on a chair in the middle of the kitchen, the sleeves of his shirt rolled up to his elbows in the summer heat. We had just finished supper. Janice stood behind him and brushed his hair while I waited beside her for my turn. "We all need a new project. Money is coming in from the mill now and the house here is all fixed up. It's time to move on." I glanced at Mom. She was smiling. I breathed easier.

In the last few months Mom hadn't been as mean. She let Janice and me play outside after supper until it was dark. The first time she did, I realized with a jolt that the harshness inside her had eased. As Dad talked, Mom lifted Ian out of the playpen and held him on her lap at the table.

"The Cartwright place is a big step up from here." Dad shifted his weight, sat up straighter, and crossed one leg over his knee. Janice pulled the brush through his hair in measured strokes. "Six acres with a view of the water. Not bad, not bad at all." He moved his head back and forth and grinned. "The old house at the top of the property needs some work. There's a one-bedroom cottage at the bottom on Fletcher Road we can rent out." He turned to us kids. "You'll all be close enough to walk to school. No more taking the school bus. Whaddaya think of that, Rob?"

At fourteen, Rob often complained about the number of stops the bus made on the way to the high school. "Can I set up a target and practice with the 22?" He pinged the tubing of the slingshot in his hands. Dad kept talking.

"It's bigger and better than here. Everything is at the bottom of the hill. Mom can send one of you kids to the store whenever she needs something. And we'll be able to watch the ferry come in." The air buzzed as Dad talked. "Rob and Sarah can even join the 4-H club. There'll be lots of room for them to raise their own calves to show in Vancouver." He talked about the move as if it was a wonderful adventure, akin to going on one of our Sunday afternoon picnics. Mom was onside. Excitement bubbled inside me. Maybe, just maybe, everything would be different now.

The road into the new property was little more than a trail. Even though Dad drove slowly, the pickup jerked in the potholes. Rob, Sarah, Janice, and I were squished together on the wooden bench in the open box of the truck. Michael and Ian were up front in the cab with Mom and Dad. Janice and I had the seats closest to the tailgate. Sarah pretended concern. "You're way too close to the back. What if the latch comes undone? Switch seats with Rob and me and move up closer to the cab so you'll be safe." It was no use arguing. Sarah and Rob always wanted the tailgate seats.

Alders and saplings formed an overhead canopy as we bumped along. Sun shone through in splotches. Dad pulled the Chev into a clearing at the end of the road and we all piled out. All I noticed were trees and blackberry bushes everywhere. Dad lifted his cowboy hat, ran his fingers through his hair, and settled his hat back down. I saw a familiar, glazed-over glint in his eyes as they moved over the land. He pursed his mouth and squinted.

Mom, in her best housedress, stood beside him with Ian on one hip and Michael holding onto her leg. The sun formed a halo around them. Dad didn't appear to notice they were with him. Mom's eyes had the same soft expression I had seen in the pictures of her before she married Dad.

A rundown house with weathered shingles crouched on the far side of the acreage. Some of the shingles were missing and black tar paper showed through the empty spaces. A half-finished verandah ran the length of the front of the house facing the ocean. Gaping holes where the windows of the porch were meant to be lent a spooky air. Gnarled apple, pear, and plum trees, with peeling bark, grew beside the house. Hard-looking green fruit hung in clusters among the leaves.

"Hey, there's a swing, our very own swing," I called out to Janice and took off at a run. The swing dangled from an apple tree. I tested it out, then raced around the property, all the way down the hill to the cottage and back up to Mom and Dad.

"Over here above the house is where I'll build the corral and the chicken coop." Dad motioned to a wall of green. Blackberry bushes reached up to the sunlight streaming through the evergreens. Their canes, as big as my arm, wrapped themselves around the trunks of the trees and dripped down from the boughs. Killer canes, I thought, waiting to reach out and tear people's flesh.

Mom sat Ian down on the grass and walked around the outside of the house. I ran inside and she followed. She had already seen the inside with Dad, when they talked to Mrs. Cartwright about buying the property. There was a back entry, a woodstove in the kitchen, a small living room, three bedrooms, and a bathroom with a stained bathtub and a toilet with no seat. Wallpaper hung in strips off the walls and patches of linoleum were missing. "Your father and his schemes." I heard pleasure in her voice. "I think we'll do just fine here. The Lord is with us. Anybody else might have been put off by the condition of the house, but we'll soon have it spruced up."

Mom relished the idea of being away from the eyes of next-door neighbors. Where we lived around the bay, the houses were all on small lots. Everyone on the street watched how our Mormon family lived—special underwear and all.

We named our new home "the house on the hill" and moved in at the end of the summer. The fruit on the trees was ripe and juicy. The forest surrounding our new property made up for losing the beach at the end of our old road. I could still see Christine and Brent at school. Dad was right. Just as he said it would be, the house and six acres was much better than living around the bay. From our living room windows, we had a view of the fishing boats and tugs tied to the government dock. On sunny days sailboats glided in the harbor.

There were three routes to school: Schoolhouse Road, an old logging road at the back of the house, and a trail through the woods at the side of our property. I took the trail. On the third day of grade two, when I was seven, I heard a quail squawking, then saw it zig zag in front of me. From what Dad had told me, it was a mother running as a decoy away from her nest of young chicks. I hunted for the nest but never found it.

A few months after we moved in, on a Saturday morning at breakfast, Dad said to Mom, "I bought us a new bulldozer. It's being delivered today." He took another bite of his toast, his eyes thoughtful while he chewed. My stomach dropped and my eyes darted to Mom. Her face was white. Her mouth opened but no words came out. We kids went quiet. I stopped eating and clenched my spoon.

"I want to clear off that bush and make a road straight up here from the cottage."

He didn't make eye contact with Mom. "I'll use the chainsaw to cut down some of the bigger trees. We might have to dynamite the stumps out. It'll sure beat using that cow trail in through the back."

Mom finally spoke. "Clarence, how are we going to pay for a new bulldozer? I've just sorted out next month's mortgage payment. There's nothing left over. You told me you'd wait, Clarence. You promised."

"I don't remember saying any such thing. We need a road up to the house. Why should we wait for it? What am I working for anyway? Gol darn it! Don't I get to make any of the decisions around here?"

"Clarence, we talked about it and you promised." I cringed at her begging.

"You promised me you'd wait. It'll only be a couple of months and then we can manage it."

"Oh, leave it alone, why doncha? Just leave it alone." Dad leapt up so fast his chair screeched over the floor. I jumped and shrank against mine. He banged the door shut on his way outside. Half his porridge was still in his bowl and his unfinished toast on his plate.

Mom choked out, "Keep an eye on the boys, please," and re-treated to her bedroom. Heaviness welled up inside me. My happiness was too good to last. Dad was back to spending money we didn't have, and Mom was left to sort it all out. Nothing had changed.

Baptism

JANICE WAS BAPTIZED in the ocean on a Saturday evening in July the summer after her eighth birthday. The water was warm then. Elder Williams and Elder Reach came over from Vancouver. Dad took Janice with him to the ferry to pick them up. I watched from the kitchen window as the truck pulled out of the driveway. "Why does Janice get to go with Dad to the ferry? It's not fair." Mom didn't answer. She opened the oven door and heat blasted into the sweltering kitchen as she slid five pans of bread dough onto the bottom rack. "Why do I have to stay home? Why?"

"I need you to help me here. You're my best little helper. Besides, it's Janice's special day." She eased the oven door closed and stood up, one hand on the small of her back. Every day was Janice's special day, but I couldn't say that to Mom. If I did she would take off her slipper and whack me.

After supper, the whole family dressed in Sunday clothes and piled into the pickup. Dad, the elders, and Rob wore suits. Michael and Ian wore clean pants and shirts. Mom and we girls wore dresses. "Why can't I wear my bathing suit and go swimming?" I asked Mom before we got dressed. It was a waste to go to the beach on a hot summer evening and not go in the water.

"Don't be silly and stop asking. A baptism is neither the time nor the place. Hurry up and get dressed." She shoved me toward my bedroom door.

The elders, both of them short and skinny, had laughed and joked with me in the afternoon, but as they squished into the cab with Mom and Dad, their faces were serious and grown-up. They carried books of Mormon scripture. The rest of us sat on the bench in the back. Dad drove the twenty minutes to Gower Point beach and parked at the end of the road. No one was in sight. We followed him down a narrow trail overgrown with wild roses. Birds chirped and twittered. When we reached an open stretch of beach enclosed on either side by bushes, Dad disappeared behind a bush on one side and Mom took Janice to the other side.

I followed the elders to the logs at the high tide line. A few yards below, the ocean lapped over smooth boulders and a thin skim of white foam surged back and forth. Rob and Sarah picked up pebbles and skipped them across the water.

"I've never been so close to an ocean before." Elder Reach's voice was filled with awe. He gazed at the water and pushed his glasses up on the bridge of his nose. "Where I come from, in Nebraska, we're about as far from the ocean as a person can get." He pronounced his words with a slow drawl.

Elder Williams made an indentation in the sand with the toe of his black dress shoe. "You haven't seen anything until you've seen dunes. I grew up next to mountains of sand in Oregon."

I couldn't imagine living away from the ocean. I untied my running shoes, took off my socks, and waded into the water while Michael and Ian turned over rocks. Dad came out of the bushes in a pair of white trousers and a white dress shirt. Janice had on a short white dress. We stood in a circle, Michael on one side of Mom and Ian on the other. A hush fell over the beach. "Will you lead us in a song and prayer?" Dad asked Elder Williams, the senior companion of the two missionaries.

Elder Williams hummed for a moment in the tune of "Teach Me to Walk in the Light" and began to sing: "Teach me to walk in the light of his love, Teach me to pray to my Father above . . ." I shivered at the timbre of his pure, clear voice in the evening air.

Dad held Janice's hand and guided her over the boulders into the water. His bare feet teetered on the round stones until he was waist deep. The water sucked his pants against his legs, and the skirt of Janice's dress swirled around her. Dad put his left arm behind her waist and smiled down at her. I heard him whisper, "Are you ready?" She held her nose closed with her thumb and finger and nodded.

Holding up his right arm bent at the elbow, Dad recited, "Having been commissioned by Jesus Christ, I baptize you in the name of the Father, and of the Son, and of the Holy Ghost. Amen." He leaned her back, with her eyes facing the sky, all the way under the water. Her long brown hair fanned out in strands. When he pulled her back up, her hair plastered against her head and her dress sucked onto her skin. They waded back to the beach. Janice's teeth were chattering and salt water dripped from her dress.

As my eighth birthday approached, Mom reiterated in her Sunday school lessons, "You need to be baptized to become a Mormon. Children are baptized at eight because they're considered old enough to understand the difference between right and wrong. When you're baptized, all your sins will be washed away." I didn't have any say in whether I *wanted* to be baptized. Mom and Dad had promised me to the church before I was born.

I learned to parrot the thirteen articles of faith of the LDS church. They were printed on the back of a card small enough to hold in my hand. On the front was a picture of the spires of the Salt Lake City temple set against a brilliant blue sky. The thirteen statements, written by Joseph Smith, outlined the basic teachings and ordinances of the church. I had no idea what the words meant. When I could reel the statements off from memory, Mom and Dad smiled at me, one of the few times they did.

I had heard Dad tell the missionaries during one of their weekends with us, "Most children are just naturally obedient to the gospel. If a child is strong-willed, sometimes it's necessary to break their spirit to it." A chill had zapped through me. I'd heard him say the very same thing about breaking a horse to the halter. Could he read my mind? Was he aware of what I thought about the church but didn't dare show? I was terrified of what he would do to me if he knew. My spirit rebelled at sitting through endless hours of church meetings when we went into Vancouver. And when we had Sunday school at home, all I wanted to do was play outside with my friends. If Dad knew how much I hated church services, what would he do to change my feelings about them? How was it possible to change how another person thought and felt? I didn't dare ask. Fear overruled my curiosity.

My curiosity about life and God wasn't answered in the thirteen articles of faith or in the Sunday school books Mom read to us. On my meanderings in the woods, questions came to me. Where did the feelings inside me come from? How did thoughts get into my mind? The trees and moss didn't answer with words. Instead, they drew close around me, cradling me with a sense of care that had no language. I gazed up at the night sky sprinkled with stars and a feeling of smallness, of holiness, flooded through me. In the black stillness, one question after another surfaced. What made me different and separate from my friend Christine? What made me feel like me and not someone else? What was my soul? What did it look like?

I was baptized at the church on 41st Avenue in Vancouver on a Saturday afternoon in the winter. The ocean was too cold for a baptism. Mom and Dad brought the whole family. Before we drove to the chapel, they stopped at a shoe store and bought me a pair of black patent-leather shoes and white, popcorn bobby socks, the same as some of the girls in my grade three class at school wore. I never dreamed that I would ever own a pair myself. The shoes I wore were sturdy brown leather that Mom ordered from the catalog at the beginning of the school year. She traced my feet on a piece of paper to measure the size.

The baptismal font was in a room off the hall behind the chapel. The font, filled with water, was round and tiled in miniature tiles with flecks of gold. It was big enough for two people to stand in with a little space around them. There were steps into the water from change rooms on either side. Rows of metal folding chairs formed a semicircle facing the font. Everyone who came to the service was dressed in their Sunday clothes. I sat with Mom and Dad in the back row. I had practiced for today: I lay in the water at the beach, held my nose, and let the ocean wash over me. But though I had practiced, I still trembled.

Before the first baptism, there was a hymn and a prayer. One of the priesthood holders gave a talk about how special baptism was. Those who were baptized would join God's only true church here on earth. Two priesthood holders stood to one side of the font to watch each baptism and make sure every part, including the clothing, of the children baptized was completely covered by water. If even a tiny bit of their clothing floated on the surface, they had to be submerged again.

Mom helped me change in one of the rooms beside the font. I wore the white dress that Janice had worn the year before. The change room smelled dank and mildewy. The reek of chlorine from the water in the font burned my nose. Dad changed in another room into the clothes he had worn to baptize Janice. I walked down the steps of the font in my bare feet. Tepid water pushed my dress up around my waist. Holding it against my legs, I waded over to Dad with my heart pounding in my ears. The people watching were a blur. Dad put his arm behind my back, held up his right arm, waited while I pinched my nose, and recited the baptismal prayer as he had for Janice. The water closed over me.

Back in the change room, I pulled on my new socks and a cold wetness seeped through to my feet. My baptismal dress had dripped water all over the floor and I'd stood in it. "Here, stand still." Mom grabbed my arm. "Let's get those wet socks off you and put your old ones back on."

"No, I'm not taking them off." Wet or dry, my new socks were on my feet to stay. I would carry the shoes. Mom didn't argue. The bottoms of my wet socks squelched on the carpeted floor as I walked down the hall and into the chapel. Dad, with two other priesthood holders, cupped his hands around my head and said a prayer to give me the gift of the Holy Ghost. I was now supposed to have an invisible male spirit inside me, telling me without words to be good when I wanted to do something bad.

I didn't feel any different, and no voice spoke to me. As Dad prayed, there was only the warmth of six hands pressing on my head. After Dad said amen, I slipped back to my seat beside Mom and watched the clock on the wall, anxious for the service to be over. All I thought about on the ferry ride home were my new shoes and the instructions from the salesman: "To keep the shine and the leather soft, rub vaseline on them with a cloth." I imagined dipping a soft cloth into a container of vaseline and rubbing it in circles onto my shoes. Monday, I would wear them to school and show all my friends.

Mom and Dad had spent money on fancy shoes and socks to commemorate something that was important to them, but not to me. I didn't want to get into trouble by telling them that while my body went through the motions and my mouth said the words they wanted me to say, my spirit hadn't been broken to the gospel. A weight pressed on my chest, as if I had done something wrong that I couldn't tell anyone about. Deep in my heart, I knew I was a fraud.

Secrets

"WHAT ARE YOU DOING IN THE HOUSE? I told you to stay outside and take care of the boys. Can't I have even one minute to myself?" I skidded to a halt in the doorway of Mom and Dad's bedroom. A small suitcase was open on the bed. From the door, I glimpsed blue paper lining in a diamond-shaped pattern. Laid out on the bedspread was a long white dress and a pair of white trousers. On the pillows were two dark green aprons covered in intricate embroidery.

The anger in Mom's eyes stunned me. I wheeled and ran outside. Everything I had dashed in to tell her washed away in a flood of shame. I had seen something Mom didn't want me to see. It must be seriously secret for her to be so annoyed. Heaviness churned inside me as I sat on the swing beside the vegetable garden next to the house and kicked at the worn patch of dirt under my feet. What were the white dress and green embroidered aprons for? And why was Mom so mad at me for catching a glimpse of them?

I shielded my eyes with a hand against the spring sun and checked out the lettuce in the garden. Mom had kept me off school to take care of Michael and Ian. They hooted with laughter as they tried to teach their black Lab pups, Popeye and Pluto, over by the woodshed, how to sit up and beg. The dogs yelped every time the boys held their front paws up. Their claws tore at the boys' trousers. Mom wouldn't be happy. How soon would it be before Popeye and Pluto went over the hill with Dad and his shotgun? I couldn't bear to think about it.

My mind skittered back to the clothes I'd seen on the bed.

77

Church members didn't wear white clothes at services. I had never known anyone to wear an embroidered green apron. The secret clothes had to have something to do with God's perfect plan Mom often referred to but never fully explained. "When you're old enough to understand, you'll find out everything you need to know," she said every time I asked her questions that she didn't want to answer. If I heard lowered voices, I listened intently, while pretending not to.

There were mysteries in the church, secrets so secret that they were only whispered about. I knew about one—blood atonement, which was having your blood spilled to atone for your sins so you could go to heaven. I'd heard Mom talk to Dad about blood atonement happening in the church in Utah.

The summer before was the first time I had any inkling that there were other secrets. Aunt Letty and Uncle Barry and my cousins Monica and Marcia from Salt Lake visited us. The day they arrived, I waited outside in the yard and practiced with Rob's yo-yo. When their car, a Buick, pulled into the driveway, I ran out to meet them. Hitched behind the Buick was a shiny travel trailer that they slept in. Uncle Barry, Dad's youngest brother, got out of the car, tilted his head back, and laughed. Aunt Letty crushed me against her pillowy roundness. Monica and Marcia, close in age to Rob and Sarah, disappeared to the beach with them without even coming into the house.

Aunt Letty was different than Mom. That night after supper, she pushed her chair away from the table and pulled Monica onto her lap. She talked with her arm around my cousin's waist while Monica rested her head on her mother's shoulder. Mom never pulled Sarah onto her lap or any of us younger kids. I'd only ever seen her do it with the boys when they were babies. I kept an eye on Aunt Letty and Monica, unable to stop watching their amazing behavior. Uncle Barry was different too. He laughed and teased as if he didn't have any worries. Whenever he was next to Aunt Letty, he would slip his arm around her waist and pull her close. Dad never did that with Mom.

The second day in the afternoon, Dad took Uncle Barry to the sawmill. Mom and Aunt Letty, in the kitchen, filled jars with ripe apricots. Outside, I picked up our cat Fred and sat on the back steps. Mom and Aunt Letty's voices and their laughter flowed through the screen on the open kitchen door. As soon as I heard the word polygamy, I nudged closer to the door.

"Can you believe it?" Mom said to Aunt Letty. "He had a special bed made that was big enough for all of his wives to sleep in with him." Her voice rose to a high, anxious note. A picture of the wives in white nightgowns lined up in bed on either side of their one husband fixed itself in my mind. At nine I knew nothing about sex between a man and a woman. "Thank goodness we don't have to deal with polygamy in the here and now." Mom was relieved, as if she'd escaped a terrible ordeal.

"I can't imagine what I'd do if Barry wanted to take another wife." Aunt Letty's voice was thoughtful.

Their talk drifted to Mom's regret about not living closer to a church congregation, and then to the temple. "I worry that I'll forget the passwords and gestures I need to remember," Mom said. I listened harder and pulled Fred against my chest to muffle his purring. "You're lucky you live close to the temple in Salt Lake. You can go as often as you want. There's no danger of forgetting what you need to remember. Every so often, I remind myself to go over everything in my mind. I worry sometimes that I won't even remember my secret name."

What? Mom had a secret name? What was it? And why hadn't she ever mentioned it? I didn't know who Mom was at all. A mysterious world existed behind the doors of the temple. What went on in there?

Sitting on the swing and kicking at the dirt, I thought about the pieces of Mom's secret. The white clothes and embroidered aprons from the suitcase on the bed had to be what Mom and Dad wore at the temple. After they dressed in the clothes, what came next? The passwords and gestures? When and how did Mom use her secret name? What did she need it for? Did Dad have one too?

He must have. I was sure I would get into trouble if I asked Mom anything about the passwords or her secret name.

I kept my eyes and ears open but never learned more about Mom and Aunt Letty's conversation, until years later. As an adult, reading Deborah Laake's *Secret Ceremonies* and Judy Robertson's *Out of Mormonism*, I learned of the horror that went on in the temple that Mom longed to visit. The significance of that knowledge was far more disturbing to me than finding out for the first time that Mom and Dad had sex. Mom and Dad were in too deep to ever get out. I immediately understood the trajectory of my life, why Mom and Dad were lost to me before I was born, and why their loyalty was to the church and not their family.

Leaving Gibsons

IN 1960, THE SPRING I turned ten, I took the washed-out logging road home from school instead of the trail. The road started at the end of Shaw Road and wound through the woods and down the hill into the back of our property. An abandoned car left to rust sat inside our property line. Wire springs and stuffing poked out of the upholstery. On rainy days Michael and Ian played in the car.

I dawdled on my way to the house, stopped, and checked out the car. On the backseat was a tangled mess of straps and metal spurs. My heart sped up. Strangers must have come onto our property and dumped it. Were they still around? I started to shake. Mom had warned me about strangers. "Run. If a stranger approaches you, run, and don't you ever take candy from them. Just get away fast." I tore through the trees, not stopping until I was safe in the house.

As soon as Dad got home from work, he followed me back up. He peered into the car, shook his head, and made a tsk sound between his teeth. "Climbing equipment. It's got B.C. Telephone stamped onto the leather. Nothing for you to worry about. Skedaddle on back to the house. I'll be there in a minute."

Dad came through the kitchen door and stared straight at Rob. "There's some gear in the old car. We need to talk." Rob's face went white and his Adam's apple moved up and down. I knew then that he was the one who had dumped the gear in the car. If I had known it was him, I would never, ever, have told Dad. A sick feeling moved from my stomach into my chest. Rob loved me. He told me silly jokes and I could ask him anything, even though he sometimes wouldn't tell me the answer. I had betrayed him.

Dad and Rob went outside. They were out there a long time. I listened for shouting and didn't hear any. Now that Rob was seventeen, Dad treated him as if he was just about a grown-up. When Rob received the Mormon priesthood at twelve, he joined the special brotherhood Dad belonged to.

Rob phoned his buddy Pete. They had taken the equipment from one of the open vans at the Cedars Motel, across from the high school, to go tree climbing. The spikes weren't long enough to dig into the bark. After Rob came home from school the next day, he said to me, "Stop looking so worried. The guys just laughed when we took it back. They didn't even care." It didn't end there.

Mom and Dad had private talks with Rob in his room. Rob had given up on the 4-H club the year before, and there was nothing for him to do in Gibsons except hang out in the bush with his friends. Mom and Dad bought a record player, and Rob and Sarah invited their friends over on Saturday nights. The whole house shook as they blasted music and jived in the living room to songs by Pat Boone, Peggy Lee, and Johnny Ray. They weren't allowed to dance to music by Elvis Presley. I asked Mom why not and she wouldn't tell me. Rob wouldn't either. All he would say were those words that had become so familiar: "You wouldn't understand, wait until you're older. I'll tell you then."

One Saturday morning as I was setting the table for breakfast, Rob staggered out of his bedroom. His face was pale. Dad was up at the corral milking the cow. Mom sniffed. "You were drinking last night, weren't you? When you came in I heard you stumble. Good thing your father didn't wake up. I can smell liquor fumes on you." Rob didn't answer. "After all we've taught you about right from wrong. I'm so disappointed in you. What would your Heavenly Father say?" Mom leaned against the counter and wiped her eyes with the bottom of her apron. My insides quaked. Rob sidled out the back door and headed down the hill to his job at the bakery. He was smart to get away before Dad came in with the milk.

The invitations to Rob and Sarah's friends and the dancing in the living room stopped. Rob wasn't allowed to go anywhere except school and his job at the bakery. When Dad got home from work each day, Mom pulled him into their bedroom. I paused in the hallway outside their closed door, poised to run if the door opened. All I heard were fragments of conversation: ". . . nothing for us here . . . got to face it . . . church in Vancouver . . . if only we were there . . . so much better . . ." Mom's voice was low, Dad murmured occasionally.

I heard enough to realize that Mom was trying to persuade Dad to move into Vancouver. An air of foreboding seeped into the house. Uncertainty and worry moved through the walls. Dad had closed the sawmill down a few months before. New operations, big enough to outbid him for a stand of timber, had squeezed him out. He worked in Sechelt clearing land with one of his bulldozers and could probably find work doing that anywhere.

"We need to be close to the church," Mom told us kids before she and Dad drove to the ferry one Friday after Dad finished work. "Dad and I are going to look at an acreage with a house in Richmond, close to Vancouver. We'll stay for the weekend at the Wilsons and go to church with them on Sunday." Her voice was light. She wore pink lipstick, her best dress with the flared skirt, and her sparkly broach pinned onto the shoulder. Dad wore his suit and fedora. He was unusually quiet. Mom did all the talking.

"Being close to the church will be wonderful. There'll be church services to go to every Sunday and during the week, dances for Rob and Sarah on the weekends, and wholesome activities and outings with young people who share our beliefs." I could think of nothing worse. "I'm trusting you all to behave yourselves while we're gone. Rob and Sarah, take turns milking the cow. Be careful not to get anything in it when you strain it. The rest of you, listen to what Rob and Sarah tell you. And no fighting."

Michael, Ian, Janice, and I clustered around Rob and Sarah in the living room. They slumped on the chesterfield, misery etched on their faces. "There's no way I want to leave Gibsons," Rob said. "I've got everything going for me here. I'm earning good money at the bakery. There's absolutely nothing for me in town."

"How do they expect us to make new friends?" Sarah wailed. "All our friends are here. I'm going to hate it. I am just going to hate it!" She burst into tears and ran into our bedroom, and I heard the springs squeak as she threw herself down on her bed. She did the same thing when the weekly letter from her boyfriend Rick, on Vancouver Island, wasn't at the post office. They had met the year before when she and Rob were in the 4-H club and went to a competition in Vancouver.

Mom and Dad came home late Sunday night after I was in bed. Monday morning at breakfast Dad announced, "We found a place in Richmond that will do. It's on a decent acreage. The house hasn't been lived in for a few years and needs a bit of work." He cleared his throat. "There's a small church congregation about a ten-minute drive away that meets in rented buildings. The big church, on 41st, is only a half-hour drive away." None of us kids spoke. I didn't feel like finishing my porridge. All I wanted to do was go back to bed, crawl under the covers, and stay there.

When the school year ended, we moved from the upstairs of the house into the dirt-walled basement that Dad had dug out with the help of a hired man. He wanted the upstairs empty while he and Mom fixed it up for sale. They painted the walls, put new plumbing in the bathroom and a new sink and counter in the kitchen, tore up the linoleum, and refinished the hardwood floors.

In the basement, the earth walls were damp with the constant trickle of seeping water. The only good thing about it was that when it was hot outside, it was cool in the basement. Mom laid rugs on the dirt floor and strung a blanket on a rope to form a partition between Mom and Dad's bed and ours. "Privacy for parents is important. It's not nice to sleep in the same room with children." I squirmed at her tone. Rob's bed was in one corner of the basement blocked off from the rest of us by a dresser. We used a chamber pot behind another dresser for a toilet.

Mom set up a makeshift kitchen, with a Coleman camp stove, on the covered back porch upstairs. We spent most of our time outside. The morning after we settled in downstairs, Janice and I sat at the picnic table on the back porch with Michael and Ian. Sarah had already left for her summer babysitting job. I had just swallowed the last few mouthfuls of toast. "Why don't you make some sandwiches and take the boys to the beach for the day?" Mom glanced at Janice and me.

"What kind?" Janice asked.

"Open up one of those cans of beans and mash them up."

I didn't mind mashed-bean sandwiches. They were better than French's mustard spread between the bread or sliced up radishes from the garden. The radish pieces dropped out if I didn't hold the bread tight together. Michael and Ian couldn't manage them at all. Sometimes that was all we had.

"Hurry up and finish your porridge," Janice prompted the boys. She and I made the sandwiches and wrapped them in creased wax paper, reused so many times it barely held together. We went down to the basement to change. "Don't forget to wear your sun hats," Mom called after us. "I don't want any of you getting sunstroke."

"Do you want to go to Atlee Beach or Armour's?" I asked Janice as I pulled on the stretched-out bathing suit that had been hers the summer before. The boys swam in their underwear. Atlees was around the bay where we used to live. Armour's was in Lower Gibsons across from the nurse's house where Ian was born. There wasn't much at Armour's. Sharp rocks. Muck. A line of floating docks. At Armour's, Janice and I dog-paddled back and forth underneath the floats in turn, while the other kept watch over the boys.

"If we go to Atlees, we can climb on the bluff," Janice said. I grabbed my towel from the end of the bunk bed. Waves of heat shimmered above the asphalt as we walked. The bottoms of my feet burned inside my running shoes. I held onto four-year-old Ian's hand and dragged him along. I had combed his blond hair into a little curl on top of his head. Five-year-old Michael barreled ahead, intent on swatting the bees that buzzed around yellow dandelions. Janice carried the lunch.

"Be careful, Michael, or you'll get stung," I called out. He kept swatting.

"Oh leave him," Janice said. "The bees aren't interested in him."

At the top of the rickety stairs leading down to Atlees, a few bicycles lay in the tall grass. I hoped they belonged to friends who had gotten to the beach ahead of us. Some of the steps to the beach were rotted. Rusted nail heads, useless now but dangerous, poked up in the empty spaces. Janice went ahead. I chose where I placed my weight and guided the boys behind me.

From the beach, an expanse of ocean stretched over to Vancouver Island, a narrow rise of land in the distance. The sun shimmered on the water in blinding flashes. With my shoes off, the rocks rolled hot under my feet. I lost track of the day. We poked at purple starfish with sticks, turned over boulders, and scrambled over the bluffs rimming both sides of the beach. Tide lapped and foamed at the shoreline. As the sun got hotter we waded and swam.

Before we left Gibsons, the summer days folded one into another. Mom let Janice and me and the boys spend just about every day at the beach. Sarah had her babysitting job and Rob worked at the bakery. A few evenings, Dad drove us all down to Gower Point beach, where we roasted hot dogs and marshmallows and ate spice cake, iced with brown sugar frosting, that Mom had baked in a tin film canister.

On our first of these supper outings, I helped Mom lay out the wieners and buns on a blanket spread over the sand. She explained the abundance of food. "I want you to enjoy our last summer here as much as you can. There won't be a beach close by when we move."

What would it be like to live where there wasn't a beach? The scent of salt water and seaweed filled me with pleasure. I loved to dig my bare feet into wet sand and make imprints of my steps. The ocean, with its ever-changing moods, was part of my soul, just as the forest that welcomed me and spoke without words. Over the next four weeks, I pushed away thoughts of our move and stayed in the moment. Loneliness, edged with despair, caught up with me at night. I tossed, unable to sleep, homesick for everything I loved before I had even said goodbye.

Mom and Dad found a buyer for the house on the hill. They didn't bother doing anything more to the dug-out basement. The last thing they finished upstairs was the floor. Dad sanded it with a rented sander from the hardware store, and Mom coated and polished the hardwood to a high sheen. The finish on the new floor shone with a rich elegance that matched the rest of the refurbished house. I ached with longing as I gazed through the door at the beauty I would never live in.

The House on River Road

"BATS! BATS!" SARAH SCREAMED, streaking out the kitchen door onto the back porch. I cowered close to Mom, covered my head with my hands, and listened for the whir of wings. The only noise was Sarah's whimpering. From the safety of the sagging porch, I peered inside. Nothing was there.

It was our first night in the house at the end of River Road in Richmond. Mom bathed Janice, Michael, Ian, and me in the laundry tub set up outside the kitchen door. Dad and Rob had taken the pickup back to Gibsons to get another load of furniture. They wouldn't be back until suppertime the next day. Mom was alone with us kids, with no vehicle and in a house with no electricity or telephone. All we had was a flashlight with weak batteries and a Coleman lantern.

As the late summer dusk set in, the house turned menacing. The dank smell of rotted wood filled my nose and made me queasy. Shadows lurked everywhere. Had Sarah seen bats or only imagined them? She sobbed over the possibility of a bat getting tangled in her long blonde hair and clawing her face. "Stop making such a fuss and put something on your head to cover your hair," Mom ordered. "I've got other things to worry about."

We bedded down in sleeping bags on the torn linoleum of the kitchen floor. There was a living room next to the kitchen and five bedrooms upstairs, but Mom wanted us all beside her. Was she as scared as we were? None of us protested. Even though Sarah had on a headscarf, she pulled the sleeping bag over her head.

"Everything is going to be fine now that we're close to the church," Mom told us as we settled beside her for the night.

"Things are going to be so different for us. We can worship in a real church every Sunday. At last we'll be part of a Mormon community." She had finally achieved her heart's desire.

Trapped inside a church every week, forced to sit for hours on a hard bench while men talked and talked, was a horrible fate to me. When we lived in Gibsons, the conferences in Vancouver a few times a year that Mom and Dad looked forward to were agony. Anytime I fidgeted, Mom reached over and thumped me hard on the head with her knuckle. I was thankful when we drove back to the ferry and home.

That first night in Richmond, I twisted from side to side on the hard floor. I drifted into sleep, then jerked awake, heart pounding, every time I heard a creak or rustling sound. It had to be a rat. When I was too tired to listen anymore, I finally slept.

The next morning in the August sunlight, Mom found a single bat attached to the corner of the ceiling in the upstairs hallway. "Take Ian outside," she said to five-year-old Michael. "Don't go any further than the driveway and stay away from the ditch. They're so deep here, cars disappear and people drown in them." Michael, dark-haired and solid, took the lead while slender, blond-haired Ian followed.

Sarah was terrified of the bat, although mesmerized at the same time. She still wore her scarf. "They carry all kinds of diseases," she said to Janice and me as we watched the boys amble down the driveway. Mom opened all the windows in the house that still had glass in them and the front and back doors. Sarah, Janice, and I positioned ourselves by the open front door at the bottom of the steps. Mom stood on a chair in the upstairs hall with a broom in her hands. She swung at the bat. It didn't budge. "Oh, oh, oh," Sarah wailed, her arms around her head. "It's going to get me."

"Stop that noise. If you can't be quiet, go outside with the boys." Sarah shut up. Mom took another swing, harder and faster. The bat dropped. It spread its webbed wings and flapped in panicked circles. "There it goes," Mom called out. She stepped clumsily off the chair and pulled the skirt of her housedress down at the waist. "It won't bother us anymore, it's flown out the window."

The house tilted on a rotted foundation on three acres of land beside the mouth of the Fraser River. A dyke kept the murky, fast-moving water from overflowing its banks. The drone of jet engines landing and gearing up for takeoff at the Vancouver airport across from us ricocheted through the air. I yearned to hear the wind singing through the trees in the forest and for the pebbled beaches and clear ocean water of Gibsons.

The second day in the house, while we waited for Dad and Rob, Mom scrubbed the walls and floors. As she worked, she hummed, "Nearer my God to thee, Nearer to thee, Even though it be a cross that raiseth me, Still all my song shall be, Nearer to thee . . ."

She didn't mind that our bathtub, painted cream and made of tin, was in one corner of the kitchen with a cover on top. We sat on it during the day. We had only cold running water from a pipe sticking up through the floor. The woodstove in the kitchen and the fireplace in the living room were the only heat sources for the house. Mom kindled a fire in the kitchen stove and cooked porridge, without any milk, for breakfast.

Sarah filled the canner kettle with cold water and hauled it over to the woodstove. She staggered as she lifted it onto the top of the stove to warm water for cleaning. Her head was still completely covered with her scarf. Mom gave Janice and me the job of scrubbing the wide Victorian woodwork around the inside doorways and window frames. "That's not clean enough," she said to me, shaking her head, when she checked the trim I had washed and scrubbed with Bon Ami until my hands stung. "Do it again." Janice got it right the first time. Mom never asked her to redo anything that she cleaned.

In the afternoon on the second day, Michael and Ian, being boys and not expected to do any housework, sat on the living room floor and rolled marbles from the high side of the sloped boards to the low side. The floor was so slanted that the marbles hit the wall with a bang. The boys shrieked with laughter every time a marble smacked into the wall.

"Stay away from the holes in the floor," Mom called out from the kitchen. "I don't want you falling through." Some of the holes exposed the supporting timbers and the dirt of the ground underneath. If we lay on the floor and peered down, we spotted bugs and spiders crawling around in the dirt and on the beams.

Dad and Rob got back at suppertime. The pickup truck was heaped high and a tarp was tied tight over the load. Dad got out of the cab, slammed the door shut, and stretched. We all crowded around him. "Aah," he yawned. "Whew. What a rigamarole. That ferry ride and the drive over here sure takes it out of a fella." He reached his arm around Mom and pulled her to him. He hadn't shaved. His chin grazed her face. She jumped back.

"Ouch. Clarence, that hurts."

"Oh come on, what's a little whisker rub, eh?" He laughed and grabbed at her.

"Clarence, stop that right now." She moved out of his reach.

Before Dad and Rob unloaded the pickup, Dad walked around the outside of the house. He crouched down every so often, examined the foundation, and shook his head. When they came into the kitchen, he said to Rob, "I knew when we bought this place we'd have our work cut out for us. The house will have to be jacked up. We'll need to put some new timbers in to shore up the foundation. First, we need to build a corral out back for the cow so we can have milk, and a chicken coop so I can bring the chickens over." Mom stiffened at the mention of the corral.

On our fourth day in the house, the beds and table were all set up. Dad drove into Brighouse, three miles away, and bought lumber. A week later after he and Rob had finished nailing together a corral, he went to an auction in Vancouver. "I'll check out what they've got in the way of calves to raise for beef cattle," he said to Mom at breakfast.

Mom's hands grabbed onto the sides of her apron. "Don't you go buying anything we don't need, Clarence. We don't have money to spare. The house needs work." My chest tightened. Oh Mom, I thought, but didn't dare say, you're wasting your breath. You know

Dad can't be trusted at auctions. Why do you keep expecting something different? Mom's face was pale and pinched all day as if she had one of her migraines.

Dad didn't come home until dark. The moment we heard the pickup rattle across the bridge over the ditch, Mom was out the kitchen door. It was raining, a steady downpour that freshened the muggy summer air and spilled out the scent of moist dirt. She didn't put on a coat or cover her hair. My stomach was quivery and I stayed in the house. Sure enough, I heard a whinny and the bang of hooves against the raised sideboards of the pickup. Dad had spent the money Mom wanted for the house—on a horse.

The Noose Tightens

TWO WEEKS AFTER we moved to Richmond, Rob pleaded his case with Dad. He paced in front of the woodstove, unhappiness etched on his face. I listened as I washed the supper dishes. "Why can't I go back to Gibsons and stay with Pete while I finish my last year of school?" His eyes were earnest. I wished Dad would let him go. Rob missed his friends and was worried that Judy, the girl-friend he had a crush on, would find another boyfriend.

"Pete's mom said I can stay with them. I can pay my own way. I've saved my wages from the bakery. They'll give me back my job, and I can always find work in the summer at the pulp mill in Port Mellon or down at the new ferry dock in Langdale." Dad lounged on a chair with his elbow on the table and fiddled with a toothpick. Rob was just about an adult.

"I wish I could say yes, but I can't. We moved to Richmond to be closer to the church. Give it a little time. You'll meet lots of nice Mormon girls at the dances they hold in Vancouver and you'll for-get all about Judy. You'll just have to trust me." Rob stomped up to his bedroom and didn't come out all night. He wasn't quite brave enough to disobey Dad. Did his obedience have something to do with the priesthood he and Dad shared and the secrets that went with it? I couldn't be absolutely sure. Rob never talked about the church. I didn't know whether he had a testimony or not.

The next morning after breakfast, as soon as Dad went outside, Sarah complained to Mom. "I hate it here. The house is filthy and disgusting and horrible. I miss all my friends. No wonder Rob's not happy. How could you and Dad move us here?" She started to cry.

Mom's face hardened. "There are more important things than

the temporal. Our life here is just the twinkling of an eye in the scheme of God's plan. I'd like where we live to be nicer too, but we'll just have to make the best of it. Being close to the church is what matters." Mom's voice rose. "Count your blessings for what you do have. There are people in the world who have far less than we do." The determination in her voice left no room for argument. Sarah hiccuped back a sob, and, as Rob had done the night before, stomped up the stairs to her room.

Sarah knew better than to say anything around Dad, although he no longer took his belt to her. Instead, he wounded her with words. He wasn't happy that she was still writing to Rick on Vancouver Island and that Rick sometimes came to visit her. I heard him say to her after supper one night, "Why are you wasting your time with him? A Mormon girl should always marry a Mormon boy. Has he agreed to take missionary lessons yet?"

Dad derived pleasure from goading her until he could get her to cry. She never learned. She tried to stand up for herself when he picked on her, but she was no match for him. I thought he treated her differently than Rob because she was a girl. It was as if belittling her and breaking her spirit was a game he needed to win. His attacks were random. Anything could set him off. His eyes lit up when he started in and he got excited. I hated it when he was mean to Sarah. There was nothing I could do other than go up to my room so I didn't have to watch and listen.

Every day before school started in September, as soon as my household chores were finished, I lay in the tall grass under the apple and pear trees beside the house and shielded my eyes against the afternoon sun. Clouds floated in an endless blue sky, uninterrupted by trees or hills. Richmond was barren and drab. My skin sweated in the August heat as I swatted halfheartedly at flies buzzing around my face and wished I was back in Gibsons.

Janice didn't mind either way. I talked to her in our room about how much I missed Gibsons. My feelings puzzled her. "I don't get why it's such a big deal to you." She talked down to me with Dad's nastiness. Maybe it was genetic or maybe she thought she was entitled to act any way she wanted because she never got into trouble for it. I had learned to move fast when we did the dishes. If she was annoyed, she'd stamp on my bare foot with her shoe. I didn't understand her viciousness or her need to hurt me. She didn't miss Gibsons; nothing had changed for her with our move. Mom and Dad still worshipped her, the same as they had in Gibsons.

In Richmond, Mom and Dad started each morning with family prayer before breakfast, an entirely new practice. We had never had morning prayer in Gibsons. I knelt on the floor beside my chair with the rest of the family while my porridge cooled in a bowl on the table. Dad usually prayed. He went on and on about everything he was thankful for and everything he wanted help with. He ended with a blessing on the food. Every so often he would pick one of us to say the prayer. When he chose me, I had it down to three sentences so I could eat my porridge before the skin formed on top:

Heavenly Father, we thank you for this food and ask you to bless it.
Please keep us all safe during the day.
In the name of Jesus Christ, Amen

There was no escape from the ritual of morning prayer. I was forced to my knees by the unspoken consequences if I didn't. Seared into my mind and imprinted in the cells of my body was the memory of Sarah protesting about home Sunday school when she was fourteen. It had happened when we lived in the house on the hill.

"Why do we have to have damn Sunday school anyway?" she had complained one sweltering Sunday morning as we gathered in the living room. "None of my friends have to." Dad exploded. He kicked over a chair with a bang and ripped off his belt. Sarah became a statue. I stopped breathing.

"Into your bedroom, now! Now! I'll teach you what's right! And I'll teach you to swear!" The door slammed shut but we heard everything. Mom stood by and said nothing. Michael and Ian were quiet.

I cringed and cried as Dad's belt thudded against the clothes on Sarah's body and slapped the bare skin of her arms and legs.

She howled. I wanted to scream, "Stop, Dad! No, Dad! No!" My voice stayed inside. What if he turned on me? I was ashamed of my cowardice. It didn't matter that I was only nine years old then. I had let Sarah down. She stayed in our bedroom all that afternoon after Dad attacked her. I crept around and didn't have the words to tell her how sorry I was.

Whenever Dad went after one of us with his belt, none of us talked about it afterward. Not the person he'd beaten or those of us who had witnessed it. We were never told not to, we just didn't. Mom never said anything either. Dad's violence stole all our voices and rotted the love in our family.

I never saw Dad beat Rob or even talk nasty to him. Yet Sarah told me that when she and Rob were younger, before I was born, Dad often went after both of them with his belt, hollering, "If you're going to act like animals, I'll treat you like animals." I never found out how old Rob was when Dad stopped beating him.

After he beat Janice and me in Gibsons, he never did it again. I learned my lesson from that one time when I was five. I still trembled when he was anywhere near me and got out of his sightline fast. He had fresh targets—my younger brothers. According to the church, he was the head of the house, God's servant here on earth, with the right to beat his children and chastise Mom as he wished.

In Richmond it was impossible to ignore the church. The coiled serpent that had slept in a corner while we lived in Gibsons was now awake. It loomed large and powerful and dominated every part of my life. Meeting by meeting, week after week, it tightened its grip and squeezed the life out of me. On Sunday in the Mormon church, everyone, not just children, was expected to go as a family to Sunday school in the morning and again in the evening for a service called sacrament meeting. On a weekday evening, there was a meeting called Mutual for teenagers, and on Saturday morning kids under twelve went to a meeting called Primary.

Richmond was a small congregation by Mormon standards. When we arrived, it had just gone from the church's designation of a branch, which is a congregation of under two hundred, to a ward. A ward is a congregation of over two hundred with enough members to fill all the volunteer positions needed to carry out the full program of the church, as mandated by Salt Lake City.

The chapel was on Blundell Road off Railway Street, a ten-minute drive from home. It wasn't the standard red brick structure that Mormons build throughout the world, but a small rented building with white clapboard siding and dark ornate pews. Beside the chapel, a two-story, gray stucco building was used for Sunday school classes, church suppers, and Relief Society meetings, the women's organization of the church.

I dreaded the first Sunday in Richmond. We all had baths the night before. Mom gave Dad, Rob, and the boys a haircut. They each took their turn on a chair in the middle of the kitchen with a plastic sheet draped over their shoulders. Black hair drifted to the linoleum as Mom trimmed and shaped using silver clippers. Whenever one of them, even Dad or Rob, shifted on the chair, she thumped them hard on the head with her knuckle. "Stop fidgeting and sit still. I don't want to nick your neck." It was the one time Mom was completely in charge, and she made the most of it.

While Mom cut their hair, I dipped an old toothbrush into a tin of black shoe polish and smeared it over their Sunday shoes. The acrid smell of polish lingered as I rubbed the leather to a high sheen with one of Dad's old work socks.

Early that first morning, as they would every Sunday, Dad and Rob went to priesthood meeting for the men and boys over twelve. When they left the house, they looked lean and handsome in their suits, white shirts, and ties. Rob had insisted on wearing a narrow, yellow tie, his unspoken protest against our new regime after Gibsons. Dad carried a tan leather briefcase and Rob carried three books of Mormon scripture under his arm. He had greased his newly cut hair with Brylcreem and combed it into a duck wave that fell over his forehead. He was as handsome as Elvis Presley. Mom and Dad let him wear his hair the way he wanted.

After the priesthood meeting, Rob drove home in the station wagon Dad had bought with money from the house sale in Gibsons. "Are you ready for the big day?" Rob teased as I scowled and climbed into the backseat to go to Sunday school. He was my ally. He was aware of how much I hated church services, although we didn't talk about it much. There was nothing he could do to help me. Rob made jokes, rather than talking, about anything that bothered him.

Mom wore her gray dress with the skirt that flared out and her special-occasion red lipstick. The church allowed women to wear tasteful makeup—it made them more attractive to their husbands. I smelled the Evening in Paris perfume Mom had dabbed behind her ears and on her wrists from a blue glass bottle. I loved the elegance of the round, flat bottle she kept out of my reach. The one time she let me touch it, it was cool on my fingers.

Sarah, Janice, and I wore our school skirts and blouses. Michael and Ian were dressed in suits that Mom had sewed on her treadle machine with material cut from Dad and Rob's old ones. As Rob drove into the parking lot alongside the stucco building, the station wagon's tires crunched on the gravel. Sunlight glinted off the front windshield and momentarily blinded me. I was stiff all over and didn't want to get out of the car. "Now remember," Mom cautioned as we rolled up the windows, "behave yourselves, and for goodness sake don't any of you do or say anything to embarrass me. Michael and Ian, make sure you use your handkerchiefs."

Mom held the boys' hands, one on either side of her, as we walked from the parking lot to the chapel where Dad waited. Women wearing cotton dresses and nylon stockings, some with babies in their arms, smiled and nodded as they grabbed hold of toddlers and pulled them out of our way. The older children and teenagers, standing outside the chapel in the summer heat, stopped talking and stared. Sarah, at sixteen, with her luxurious blonde hair, blue eyes, and curvy body, drew all the men's eyes. Men always noticed Sarah, no matter where she was.

One of the ladies at the chapel door greeted Mom. "My, what a fine family of children you have." The woman smiled with her whole face, and her eyes were warm and welcoming. "I'm Sister Baxter, president of the women's Relief Society." She shook Mom's hand. Sister Baxter was a tall woman with dark curly hair, a bit older than the other women we walked by. A purse dangled from the crook of her arm. I assumed she had positioned herself by the chapel door to await our arrival while the other women hung back. "My husband told me you were coming when he picked me up for Sunday school. He met your husband and son Rob at priesthood meeting."

Mom pushed each of us forward. When she got to me, she said, "And this is our baby girl, Maggie." I groaned inwardly. Ten years old was hardly a baby. Whenever Mom trotted me out for display, she baby-talked. I never understood why. Sister Baxter smiled at me.

"I've got a daughter your age. She'll be in your Sunday school class today. I'll tell her to watch for you. Her name is Joanne."

Inside the chapel, tall stained-glass windows filtered the sunlight and the dark, heavy wood paneling kept the heat out. Our family, which I noticed was the largest, stretched across an entire pew. The rest of the families had three or four children to our six, and most of the parents were younger than Mom and Dad.

The bishop, flanked by his two counselors, sat at the front facing the congregation. When he stood at the podium to start the meeting, his suit jacket stretched tight across his middle. An old pedal organ, played by an energetic woman, wheezed out tinny music. Another woman stood to one side of the organ with a music baton in her hand. The names and page numbers of the songs were posted on the wall beside her head. I flipped to page 52 of a worn songbook and began to sing, "Now let us rejoice in the day of salvation, No longer as strangers on earth need we roam, Good tidings are sounding to us and each nation, And shortly the hour of redemption will come . . ."

After we sang, one of the bishop's counselors opened the meeting with a prayer. The bishop gave a short talk and the sacrament was served. Rob, who held the Aaronic priesthood and was a deacon, the first level of Mormon priesthood, joined in with the other deacons. He stood with them in a row at the front of the chapel next to a table covered with a white cloth. Silver plates piled with cubes of bread, and trays of tiny paper cups filled with water, rested on the table. Each of the young men picked up a plate of bread and a tray of water and took them to the end of the pews.

As we filed out to our classes, Janice and I stuck together. Sister Baxter's daughter Joanne rushed up with a big smile and grabbed my arm. Her hair was dark and curly, identical to her mother's, and she wore a yellow, frilly dress. I bet her family was rich. She bubbled, "Mom said you're in my class and I'm supposed to show you where it is. My name is Joanne. What's yours?"

"I'm Maggie and my sister is Janice." My stomach tightened. Janice and I followed her on the boardwalk from the chapel to the stucco building. Our classroom, a small room in the basement with a painted cement floor, had no windows, but at least it was cool. There were twelve of us, girls and boys, the girls in dresses or skirts and the boys in suits, on the rows of folding chairs. The kids laughed and talked as they glanced at Janice and me out of the corner of their eyes. We sat in the back row beside Joanne. She beamed. My mouth was dry.

The kids quieted down as a tall man with red hair rushed through the door to the seat at the front and placed a stack of books on the chair beside him. His freckled face dripped with sweat. "Whew, is it ever hot. Sorry I'm late." His eyes rested on Janice and me as he wiped his face with a handkerchief. He smiled at the two of us as if we were celebrities. "My name is Brother Adderson. I spoke to your father at priesthood meeting. I'm sure your family will be a great addition to our membership." His glance took in the class. "Boys and girls, I hope you'll make our newcomers welcome."

Janice smiled, smoothed her skirt over her knees, and fluttered her eyelashes. My face flushed. I gripped the edges of the metal chair with my sweaty hands to cool them down. The class was another ordeal before I could go home. Brother Adderson paused. All the kids turned and smiled. I wished that I was anywhere but here, at church, trapped in a small, windowless room. My lips curved back in a smile.

Fast Sunday

I OPENED MY EYES and pushed past layers of sleep, then wham! The memory of what day it was hit me. I closed my eyes, dove deeper into the comfort of the bedcovers, and wished I could sleep until the next morning.

There was no rush to get up for breakfast. There was none. Nor was there any need to peel potatoes and carrots in readiness for Sunday dinner. We wouldn't be eating that meal either. The first Sunday of each month was called Fast Sunday. Members were required to fast—to go without eating or drinking, even water, for a minimum of two meals. The money families saved on food was donated to the church.

The first Fast Sunday in Richmond, as soon as Dad and Rob left for their priesthood meeting, I begged Mom in the kitchen, "Please, can't we eat just a little bit? A piece of toast maybe? Michael and Ian are starving. I'm so thirsty. Can't I have even a little sip of water? Why do we have to fast, anyway? We never had to in Gibsons."

"Stop it," Mom snapped. "Now that we're close to a church, we're going to live the way God wants us to. It's a privilege to go without breakfast and dinner. We'll have something to eat at suppertime. Stop pestering me. Go up to your room and get dressed for Sunday school." I was too afraid of what would happen to me if I disobeyed and snuck a sip of water. I was sure Mom would tattle to Dad.

Supper was a long way off. Mom's words were another bar on the prison door that clanged shut after we left Gibsons. Her logic didn't make any sense. While we starved, the money she saved on the meals that we did without, she gave to the church. It couldn't have been much, pennies maybe. Mom never told us the amount. She paid it in addition to tithing. Paying money to the church for starving wasn't what I would call a benefit. The money from Fast Sunday was supposed to go to those less fortunate. I couldn't imagine who that might be. We had to be the poorest family in the ward. I stomped up the stairs and slammed my bedroom door.

Janice was in the room we shared, getting dressed. I flounced onto my bed and watched her zip up her jumper and smooth down the skirt. She still had the sponge curlers in her hair that she had put in the night before. "I hate it, I absolutely hate it!" I fumed. "No food until supper. And not even water to drink. What are they going to think of next?"

"Why are you acting so silly?" Janice frowned and unclasped one of the curlers. "It's only two meals." I wished that I hadn't told her I was hungry. When would I learn to keep my mouth shut?

At Sunday school that morning, my empty stomach was all I could think about. My mouth was dry and parched. I licked my lips and rolled my tongue around inside to try and make more saliva. A service called fast and testimony meeting followed Sunday school. During the meeting, everyone sat quietly in the chapel and waited for members in the congregation to stand up and bear their testimony. As the silence ticked by, people coughed and babies whimpered. A toy hit the floor with a bang.

My stomach growled. I sweated and thought of my favorite Sunday dinner—golden fried chicken, creamy mashed potatoes smothered in gravy, juicy corn on the cob, and tender carrots with green peas fresh from the garden. If by some miracle we could go home for dinner right now, I would never complain about peeling potatoes and carrots again.

Finally, an older man stood up. He rested his hands on the back of the pew in front of him. All eyes turned to him. "I'm thankful for all the blessings I have in my life because of the church," he began. His voice had the same tone that Mom and Dad's had whenever they talked about the church. I tuned him out. What was my friend Christine in Gibsons doing right now? After he sat down, men, women, and children stood up one by one and talked about how much they loved the church and how they believed the gospel to be true. They all said the same thing in different ways.

"I know that Joseph Smith was a true prophet of God."

"I know the Mormon church is the only true church on earth."

"I know President McKay is a true latter-day prophet."

"I know these things to be true beyond a shadow of doubt."

There were intervals between speakers. Partway through the meeting, the salty smell of crackers and cheese wafted from the foyer at the back of the chapel. Spit started back up in my mouth. I swallowed, licked my lips, and craned my neck. A pregnant woman was nibbling on a piece of cheddar cheese. From the color, it was probably aged, the variety with a sharp, satisfying tang. The two times we visited Alberta, Dad had gone to the cheese factory and bought a heavy wheel of aged cheddar with white mesh stuck to it. Mom shared it out to make it last. Oh, how I wanted a taste of that now.

One of the mothers stood her toddler, a little boy, on the pew beside her and prompted him to speak. Haltingly, in a baby voice, he recited, "I no dis urch is twu." His mother hugged and kissed him and his father smiled. Were those tears in the father's eyes? I wanted to shake my head. The kid couldn't have had any idea what the words he was reciting meant.

At the end of the meeting, Dad drove us through an area of Richmond with unpaved roads and fields on either side. The tilled fields stretched for miles. Ian sat on Mom's lap in the front seat beside Dad, with Michael on her other side by the door. Rob and Sarah each got one of the windows in the backseat. Janice and I were crammed in the middle. I was so hungry I would have been willing to eat a banana, my least favorite fruit. I would have gladly bitten into the soft mushy pulp even though it would have squished into a blob in my mouth. We didn't have any bananas at home, and even if we had, Mom wouldn't have brought them along, let alone let us eat them now.

"I've heard about a place called Finn's Slough," Dad said as he drove. "Apparently it's at the end of Number 4 Road, next to the dyke. A whole community built over the water by Finnish settlers. Imagine that."

I was dizzy. I laid my head against the back of the seat, and as I did I brushed against Janice. She shoved her shoulder hard against mine and jabbed me in the ribs with her elbow. "Ouch. I was only trying to get comfortable. I didn't bump you on purpose. You don't have to be so mean."

"You two back there, no fighting," Dad hollered, his eyes on the rearview mirror. "Don't make me stop and take off my belt. Let's have a pleasant afternoon, all right?" I shrunk into myself, closed my eyes, and thought about the sizzle and sputter of bacon frying. I could almost taste it. I had only ever had one piece the rare time we had it at breakfast. When I grew up, I was going to eat as many pieces as I wanted.

"Take a look at those fields," Dad said. "Such rich black soil. No wonder they grow so much food. I've never seen anything like it except when I was on my mission. Did you know that the island we're driving on is made up of silt, dragged down over the centuries by the river?"

Rob and Sarah shifted in their seats. The springs underneath me moved and creaked. My eyes fluttered open. Rob and Sarah rolled their eyes at each other. Ian whimpered. "How soon can we eat, Mom? How soon can we eat?" Mom and Dad ignored him.

Michael piped up, "I'm hungry. And I'm thirsty. My stomach hurts."

Dad raised his voice. "How old do you kids think that house is?" He pointed to a small building in the corner of one of the fields, with weathered brown shingles and a black tar paper roof. A sullen silence filled the car. I thought of the bacon again.

"Now children," Mom said in a peppy voice. "Let's all have a happy time. Why don't we start counting the houses along the way? After we visit Finn's Slough, I'm hoping Dad will drive us down to Steveston."

Please let the afternoon be over and let it be suppertime. I hated the Mormon church even more than before. What kind of church asked parents to starve their kids and give the money they saved on food to the church? And what kind of parents obeyed?

Ticket to Heaven

SIX MONTHS AFTER we moved to Richmond, Dad was called by God to be second counselor to Bishop Simpson, the leader of the ward. God spoke through prayer to President Woods, the stake president and head of all the congregations in the Vancouver area, and to Bishop Simpson, telling them that Dad was their man. Bishop Simpson, along with his first counselor, Brother Jarvis, and Dad formed the bishopric that ran the programs for the ward and governed the members. A male secretary-treasurer was also called to assist. None of them were paid. The money collected from the Richmond members in tithing and donations was sent to the church headquarters in Salt Lake City.

President Woods announced Dad's calling in evening sacrament meeting the second week of February. He stood beside Dad on the podium at the front of the congregation with his hand on Dad's shoulder. The light from the fixture hanging above them shone in a halo around the two men. Dad grasped one side of the pulpit, a humble expression on his face. I could tell from the way his knuckles whitened that he was nervous. As Mom looked up at Dad and President Woods, happiness emanated from her in a blissful glow.

After the service, I stood on the frost-flattened grass in front of the chapel with my new friends, Sandy and Madeline, shivering in the thin, plaid coat Mom had bought at a rummage sale and shuffling my feet to keep warm. Sandy's stylish store-bought coat had a fake fur collar. Madeline wore her older sister's hand-me-down coat. Our breath made white puffs in the air. "So I guess you won't want to hang out with us at church anymore, eh?" Sandy asked.

"Wh-a-at?"

She and Madeline burst out laughing. "You should see the look on your face," Sandy said. "It's priceless. I was only kidding, but now that your father is in the bishopric, I thought maybe you'd act all la-de-da, as if you're too good for us."

"I don't think so."

"Okay, okay, just checking."

As second counselor to the bishop, Dad talked to members about their personal lives and interviewed them for teaching positions in the ward. He led Sunday school and sacrament meetings, blessed babies, and officiated at baptisms and funerals. He was also a home teacher who, with another priesthood holder, visited members in their homes once a month and gave them a message from the church in Salt Lake City. About the only thing Dad couldn't do was interview members for their temple recommends. Bishop Simpson and President Woods did that.

A temple recommend is an official church form that a member needs to get into the temple. The form confirms that the person is a member in good standing and worthy to enter the temple. It is good for one year and certifies that the member pays their tithing and donations, lives the Word of Wisdom, and meets all the moral, spiritual, and service requirements of the church.

With his church duties and bishopric meetings a few times a week in addition to his regular job, Dad was rarely home. I didn't miss him. Mom was left to take care of everything at home, with the help of us kids, while Dad spent his time doing the work of the Lord. She leaned on Rob and Sarah even more heavily than before. As soon as they got home from school, they started on the list of chores she had for them.

Members in the Richmond ward had instant respect for Dad when they learned he had served a mission. They were impressed, too, that he had supervised genealogy work in southern Alberta before he married Mom. Genealogy is a critical part of Mormonism. Members trace their ancestors' names, birthdates, and marriages as far back as they can find records. One of the reasons is to arrange for baptisms and marriages of dead ancestors, by proxy, during temple ceremonies.

Mom had a large book, similar to a photograph album, with diagrams that traced her and Dad's family trees. One day after school, I sat at the kitchen table and pored over it to find out how old the girls were when they were married, how many children they had, and whether there were any babies born out of wedlock. Many of the girls were as young as fourteen when they got married. I turned to Mom at the sink. "Why did the girls get married so young?"

She dried her hands and peered over my shoulder at the open page. "They wanted their daughters married off as soon as they reached puberty so they wouldn't disgrace the family with any illegitimate children. Every time Dad and I go to the temple, we take a family name and do temple work for them so they can be admitted into the celestial kingdom."

I assumed that the spirits of my ancestors, the ones who died before Joseph Smith started the church, were in the terrestrial or telestial kingdom, where non-Mormons went. I was unclear on the structure of heaven before Joseph Smith. It didn't matter whether dead ancestors had been good or evil during their life. They could even be murderers. As long as the temple work was done for them by proxy, all their sins would be washed away and they hopped up to the celestial kingdom. It didn't seem fair. They had an easier time of it than the Mormons who were alive. The dead ones didn't have to give their lives in service, promise their kids to the church, or pay money to get their ticket to heaven.

The first Sunday after Dad was called as a second counselor, he went to the bishopric meeting that followed Sunday school. The whole family waited to go home until his meeting finished. We had been at the church at nine-thirty in the morning, and it was two o'clock before Dad drove us home for dinner. I counted the time in minutes. During out wait, Mom read us church stories in one of the classrooms in the stucco building. Michael and Ian played outside. They ended up wrestling on the ground.

Rob and Sarah lounged with their feet up on the metal folding chairs and groaned every so often. Janice read a book. When I complained about being hungry, she said, "What is your problem? Why can't you just wait quietly? You can be such an embarrassment. You're so annoying." I went out to the station wagon and, even though it was cold, fell asleep with my cheek pressed against the window.

Dad invited the missionaries for dinner. I was thankful it was a Sunday we had fried chicken instead of boiled beans. While we ate, Dad laughed and joked with the two young men. I thought they were handsome in their suits and watched their every move. Both of them wore glasses. They snuck shy glances at Sarah while they listened to Dad talk.

Later, Rob stood in the kitchen with his back against the woodstove and told jokes while Sarah, Janice, and I washed and dried the dishes. Being male, Rob wasn't expected to do any of the chores in the house. Sometimes Sarah complained to Mom—she knew better than to provoke Dad. As we worked, Rob laughed out loud at his own jokes. Even though I had heard them all before, I smiled at his punchlines. He was the only one in the family other than Sarah that I trusted.

We drove back to church in the evening for sacrament meeting. It lasted an hour and a half and was a repeat of the beginning of Sunday school. Instead of dividing into classes, there were two speakers with a song in between. As children of one of the bishop's counselors, we were expected to sit up straight and listen attentively, no matter how boring the speakers or how tired we got.

I focused on the speakers' faces to make the time go faster. One of them had a mole that moved when he talked and the other had an uneven eyebrow. I was close enough to count the pinstripes on their suits, the boards of the wall behind them, and the tiles on the ceiling before I started to fidget. Rob glanced over at me and winked. I scowled back, even though I was happy that he was thinking about me. Was he as anxious for the service to be over as I was? If he was, I bet he was thinking about Gibsons and wishing he was there, back in his old life, when we didn't have to go to church all the time.

After sacrament meeting, Dad chatted with the members while Mom and we kids talked to our friends. Dad stood with his elbow resting on the tall back of the old-fashioned pew. His leather briefcase sat beside his feet and his hand jingled the change in his trouser pocket.

As part of Dad's calling, if anyone had personal problems, the bishop often asked Dad to talk to them. Dad met with them after sacrament meeting while we waited to go home and have supper. Sometimes he made an appointment for a weekday evening at the church. When he came home on those nights, I listened as closely as I dared to any details he mentioned to Mom before he went upstairs to change out of his suit.

One weekday evening, Dad talked to Brother Boyce and his eight-year-old son Josh. Brother Boyce had broken his arm hitting Josh. "Can you believe it?" Dad laughed to Mom as he loosened his tie before he went upstairs. Mom was sitting at the table with a pile of mending on her lap. Janice and I had our homework spread out across from her. The boys were in bed.

"He turned around in the car while he was driving, whacked Josh, and broke his own arm on the seat. What kind of a fluke is that?" Mom eyes widened but she didn't say anything. "I gave Josh a good talking to about acting up. Now that he's eight, he knows right from wrong. If he'd been behaving himself, his father would never have broken his arm."

The next morning after Dad left for work, I talked to Mom as she sprinkled yeast over warm water in the bread pan. "I don't think it's fair that Josh got into trouble. It's Brother Boyce's own fault he broke his arm. He shouldn't have hit Josh." Mom shook her head and walked into the pantry to get the flour.

"Your father believes in the scripture of spare the rod and spoil the child." I shuddered, thinking about Dad's idea of discipline. I stayed out of his way, but I couldn't protect Michael or Ian. A couple of weeks before, we had all been in the kitchen just before supper. Dad was at the table with the *Sun* newspaper spread out in front of him. Michael and Ian were squabbling over whose turn it was to bring in wood.

"Can't you boys ever behave yourselves?" Dad bellowed, his face flushed. The veins in his neck popped out and I started to shake. "Can't I have one moment of peace and quiet? How many times do I have to tell you? No fighting! When are you going to learn!" He leapt off his chair and tore off his belt. I stopped breathing. With each lash of Dad's belt, Michael and Ian howled in pain. Dad frothed at the mouth and danced around them. "I'll teach you to behave yourselves, I'll teach you."

"Please, Dad, stop, please stop!" I begged and screamed till my throat was sore and my voice hoarse, not caring if he turned on me, just wanting him to stop hurting my little brothers. Only when Michael and Ian were curled on the floor, whimpering in pain, past trying to escape his belt, did Dad stop.

When Sister Jensen, a newly married woman, talked to Dad with her husband about a teaching job she'd been offered, Dad counseled the couple against her accepting. "It's only asking for trouble," he said to Mom when he came home after his appointment with them. "Placing herself in the way of temptation throughout the day with men who aren't church members. She should be at home doing the work of the Lord, raising children, and honoring the commitments she made in the temple."

Occasionally, Dad got a telephone call late at night. The evening calls became more frequent when the Mormon polygamists from Bountiful, in the eastern part of the province, descended on Richmond. They were on the hunt for teenage brides to add to their collection of wives. Our family, with three girls, was one they set out to woo.

Polygamy

THE MAN ENTERED our lives on a sunburned day at the end of May when I was eleven. Dad was at his bishopric meeting after Sunday school. Mom was lingering in front of the chapel with the boys, and Rob was inside putting away the sacrament trays. Sarah, Janice, and I had decided to wait in the car in the parking lot.

As we sauntered toward the station wagon, a balding man dashed for our car with his hand outstretched. He left a young pregnant woman and a bunch of kids in front of the building next to the chapel. He smiled straight at Sarah and reached for the door handle. He was fat and had pointy little teeth.

"Let me do that for you," he said with an oily snigger. My stomach turned over. His tone of voice was the same kind the boys at school used when they told dirty jokes and laughed during recess. Why was he talking to her like that? Sarah was only sixteen and he was an old man.

He wasn't a member of the Richmond congregation. I had never seen him before. His hand on our car door and the way he ogled and talked to Sarah were all wrong. It happened so fast, yet unfolded in slow motion. Sarah's eyes widened. Her face reddened and she climbed into the backseat without saying anything. Janice and I followed. The man shut our car door and faded back to the woman and children. The woman had long hair; most of the women in the ward wore their hair short.

"That was weird," Janice said. "What a creepy man. He's a stranger and he touched our car door. Oooh. What's the matter with him anyway?"

"I think he's got a crush on you," I said to Sarah. "But he's old

117

enough to be a grandfather."

"Y-u-u-k!" She held her nose and screwed up her face. We burst out laughing. I laughed until my stomach hurt and I felt safe again. We didn't unroll the windows to let the heat out of the car until we were sure that the man was gone.

None of the men at church flirted with Sarah, though they might glance at her. Everyone thought she was beautiful, including me. The missionaries made excuses—dropping off church books, asking for help to organize a young people's event—to come over during the week after she got home from school. The air sparked with electricity when they were around her.

At Sunday dinner that day, Mom passed Dad the platter of fried chicken. "Those two families who were here from the Creston area this morning, did the men come out to priesthood meeting before Sunday school?" She held onto the platter while she waited for his answer. Sarah, Janice, and I glanced at each other, then down at our plates.

Dad shook his head. "No. I never got a chance to meet them. They were out of the chapel before I could introduce myself. I had to go right into my meeting." He speared a drumstick with his fork, put it on his plate, and passed the platter to Rob.

"There's something funny about them," Mom said. I pictured the man rushing over to Sarah and the young woman's pregnant belly while she stood and watched blankly.

"What do you mean? I didn't notice anything from the front."

"I don't think they're mainstream Mormons." Mom lowered her voice. "The men are too old to have such young wives. Both of the women wore shapeless dresses and had long hair." She bit her lip.

"If they come back, I'll talk to them and find out."

That evening, the people we had seen in the morning were at sacrament meeting: the man who had opened our car door and the young woman and children with him, plus the older man and his family Mom had noticed. A middle-aged woman was also with them. She wore a blue dress that came halfway between her knees and ankles, and her hair was twisted into a bun. She wasn't wearing any makeup. They all sat together in the back rows of the chapel. I kept glancing at them; I couldn't stop myself.

After the service, I hung around on the grass in front of the chapel and watched Dad introduce himself and shake hands with the two men. He smiled and chatted, just as he did with all the men in our ward, while the young women and children stood off to the side. Mom talked to the woman in the blue dress. On the drive home she said to Dad, "What did I tell you? I was right, wasn't I?" She was smug, but I noticed a thin edge in her voice. "They're from Bountiful. I knew it, I just knew it." Dad kept his eyes on the road.

I knew about polygamy in the church from the stories Mom had told, but I had never heard polygamy talked about at church. The fundamental Mormons believed that by practicing polygamy they were being true to the teachings of Joseph Smith. The more wives the men had, the more blessings they would have in heaven. They maintained that they were living God's gospel here on earth.

The two men and their wives from Bountiful were reminders of the unspoken controversy that lurked below the surface of mainstream Mormonism. Joseph Smith had introduced polygamy as part of the founding doctrine of his church. Dad rarely talked about his Mormon grandfather and his two grandmothers or that other ancestors were also polygamous. Mom kept quiet about hers.

Mom believed, in theory, that polygamy was ordained by God, although she was thankful as a mainstream Mormon that she didn't have to share Dad with other women. I doubt she had any reason to think about it. I had no idea whether she ever worried that Dad might want to marry a younger woman as a second wife.

"The older woman is the first wife of one of the men," Mom said to Dad on the drive home. "She told me it was wonderful living plural marriage. She works as a nurse, while the second wife takes care of the house and the children. She invited us to come up to Creston and stay. I was polite to her, but that's the last thing I'd ever want to do."

For a moment, I thought she was going to cry. I held my breath and hoped that what she had said hadn't made Dad angry. I hated it when they were nasty to each other, although Dad never hit Mom. "I'll talk to the bishop. If they come back, we'll keep an eye on them. Don't go getting your knickers all in a knot. It's probably nothing."

None of us girls had told Mom about the man who opened our car door for Sarah. I didn't want to be the one; Mom was upset enough already. It wasn't the kind of thing any of us would ever talk to Dad about. That night, I sat on the end of Sarah's bed and talked to her. "What if Dad decides to become a fundamentalist Mormon?" I whispered, half-expecting Dad to be listening outside the door. "I couldn't stand it if he gave you to that disgusting old man as his wife. What if he decides to give Janice and me away too?"

"No, no, he would never do that. He's got too much going for him here in the ward. All that matters to him is being in the bishopric. Besides, Rick has already asked me to marry him. There's nothing for you to worry about, honey. Dad's not going to give you away." She patted my hand. "I'm leaving home soon and I'll be out of Dad's reach." Sarah was registered with a business college to take typing and shorthand. She had a special scholarship for students who couldn't afford to pay. "As soon as I have a secretarial certificate, I can find a job."

That night, I woke with a start in the middle of a dream. In the dream Sarah, dressed in a long white gown, stood beside the old man who had opened our station wagon door for her. He had his arm around her shoulder and there was a grin on his face. Janice and I stood off to the side, both of us dressed in the same kind of white gown.

The families from Bountiful were back the following week for Sunday school. After the service, the men mingled with the men of our ward in front of the chapel, and the older woman chatted with the women members. The young wives stood to one side with their kids and waited. The same old man pushed close to Sarah beside me in the crowd. The skin on his neck hung loose. I shuddered. He smiled and reached his hand out to shake Sarah's. She pretended not to notice. He kept smiling and moved closer. I checked around for Mom. She wasn't in sight. I was the only one who appeared to notice.

Sarah moved away and headed for our station wagon. The man ran panting after her and made it to our car door in time to wrench it open before she got there. She climbed in, averting her eyes. My stomach was queasy. I wanted to do something to protect Sarah, but what? A few cars away the man's pregnant wife, a baby on her hip, a diaper bag over her shoulder, and two toddlers clinging to her legs, struggled to open their car door. She had a blank expression on her face as she focused on her kids. She didn't look over at our station wagon. It wasn't right. How could her husband fawn over Sarah while ignoring his wife's struggle with their children and the car door?

The following week, the telephone calls in the evenings for Dad began. The men from Bountiful, with their talk of God's revelations to Joseph Smith on plural marriage, had stirred everyone up in the ward about which doctrine was true. "We have to accept what the prophet today tells us through revelation," I overheard Dad say during one of the calls. "The prophet's latter-day prophecy supersedes scripture in the Doctrine and Covenants. If you're uncertain, you need to fast and pray until you have no doubts." He had to be talking about polygamy.

Sometimes Dad got out his church books and read from them over the telephone. During one of the calls he started yelling. "Listen. It's just something you're going to have to accept on faith." He slammed down the receiver and said to Mom, "It's plain stupidness, all the talk about polygamy. Everyone is getting heated up about nothing. It's a big waste of time arguing about it."

I was sure Mom was relieved to hear that Dad didn't agree with polygamy in the here and now. I had heard her talking to someone about it on the telephone. "Practicing polygamy would be the ultimate test of faith. Supposedly, in the afterlife we'll have a fuller and more complete understanding."

If Dad did decide to marry more wives, what would Mom do? I didn't want to think about it; it was too awful. I had learned what a man and woman do to have children when they get married. The thought of Dad doing that with other women besides Mom made my skin crawl. It was bad enough thinking of him doing it with Mom.

Whenever the subject of plural marriage came up at home, Mom said to me, "Mormon scripture says that in the afterlife, seven women will cling to the coattails of one man." Was she trying to prepare herself? I had heard her tell my aunt Letty that she was relieved she didn't have to practice it in the here and now. Aunt Letty had agreed with her. Whenever Mom explained polygamy to me, she said it was a hardship for the men. "It's difficult enough for a man to take care of one wife. Imagine what a burden it would be for him if he had to take care of more."

What she said didn't make any sense to me—there had to be more to it, something she wasn't telling me. In her stories of the Mormon pioneers who practiced polygamy, it was the wives and children who took care of the farms, not the men. The men spent their time working as missionaries for the church and searching out new wives to have more children with. The woman in the blue dress from the Creston area had told Mom that she left her children with another wife while she went out and earned money as a nurse. She didn't get to stay home with her children.

I was sure, too, that men would enjoy having sex with more than one woman if God gave the okay. I understood the pull that happened between a man and a woman. I was breathless around some of the missionaries, following them after services to be near them and thinking about them after I came home. Standing close to them made me quivery, but they were young and handsome, not old and ugly like the men from Bountiful.

Sarah was the only one I could talk to about polygamy. "I don't trust Dad," I told her in her room after another sacrament meeting. I didn't want the old man anywhere near her. And if Dad gave her to him, where would that leave Janice and me? We would soon be old enough to be married off too. What if Dad gave us all away?

"You've got nothing to worry about. I heard the man ask Dad if he could marry me. Dad yelled at him. He was really mad." But what if Dad changed his mind? He did that sometimes after he calmed down from one of his rages.

The families from Bountiful came back to church one last Sunday. The men never went to priesthood meeting. Instead, they attended the regular services that were open to the public.

The following week, Dad, dressed in his suit with his briefcase full of church books, went over to Bishop Simpson's house. He was gone all night. When he came home in the morning, I was in the kitchen making a peanut butter sandwich to take to school. His face was grayish and he was quiet. I got the jitters.

Had Dad changed his mind about polygamy? Was he going to give Sarah away after all? Was the bishop trying to persuade Dad not to do it? After he went up to his bedroom to change into his work clothes, I asked Mom, "What was Dad doing at the bishop's house all night?"

"He was meeting with him and his wife." That was all she would tell me.

Dad went over to the bishop's house again a few nights later. His face was bleak. Mom was quiet after the door closed behind him. Something had to be wrong for Dad to go over twice. I burned with curiosity. When Dad came home just before breakfast the next morning, his body sagged and there was a defeated expression on his face, the same as the first time he had been away all night. Before I left for school, I screwed up my courage and asked Mom, "Why did he go over again?"

"It's nothing you need to concern yourself about. It's ward business that's got nothing to do with you. Get yourself off to school or you'll be late. Catch up with the boys and make sure they don't dawdle." Her lips closed in a tight line.

I cornered Rob in his room that afternoon. Mom always told him everything and Dad talked to him too. "Don't you dare say anything to anyone. It's got nothing to do with Dad. Bishop Simpson wants to practice polygamy. Dad was over at his house all night arguing doctrine with him. He wasn't able to get him to change his mind. The bishop is determined it's the scriptural thing to do. Sister Simpson is hysterical. She's going to leave him and take their children with her."

My breath stalled in my chest. Mom and Dad had moved from Gibsons, where we were the only Mormons, to Richmond to be part of a church congregation. The stable foundation they had counted on to rescue our family and keep us all righteous had just cracked wide open.

Excommunicated

HUGH BOYD JUNIOR HIGH was dizzying after elementary school. The building was two stories high with lockers on either side of endless hallways. Each of my classes was in a different part of the school. As Madeline and I stood on the sidewalk in front of the school, a group of laughing grade nine boys jostled against us. "Sorry, sorry," they chorused and kept going.

"They did that on purpose," Madeline complained. "They think they own the school. I'll bet they wouldn't push any of the grade eight or grade nine girls out of their way." How rude, yet how sure of themselves the boys were in their little gang. In the three days I had been at the new school, I was acutely aware of my black-rimmed glasses and the hand-me-down skirt and white blouse I had worn every day.

On our walk to the bus stop, I turned to Madeline. "What happened yesterday afternoon when you went over to the bishop's house?"

"Not much. I played games with Wesley and Tina and then read to them before I put them to bed. Sister Simpson has started work as a receptionist in a real estate office and the house is for sale. You heard she's stopped coming to church?"

"Everybody's heard. I still can't believe it." I shook my head. "They were the perfect family."

"The bishop wasn't at the house. None of his clothes were in the closets. I checked. I feel sorry for Sister Simpson and the kids." Madeline loved children. She loved babysitting, more because of the kids than the money she earned. "And I think Sister Simpson's started drinking."

"What? No. Really? Are you sure?" Drinking was forbidden by the church. Mom said only low class people did it. I would never have repeated the low class part to Madeline, though, because her father drank. He wasn't a Mormon. He had started drinking years ago, before her older sister was born, while he was away during the war.

"I peeked in all the cupboards, and there were liquor bottles in the one over the fridge. I always check just in case there's any cookies or chips hidden out of the kids' reach. There's never been any liquor bottles in that cupboard before."

"Maybe she just got it to serve to company."

"No." Madeline shook her head. "She smelled kind of stale before she left. It's the same smell Dad has. I'd recognize it anywhere. And she's lost weight. I'm sure she's not eating."

I believed Madeline, although it was hard to take in. Sister Simpson wore tasteful makeup and peach-colored suits, and she had her blonde hair done every week at the hairdresser's. She had taught a Sunday school and Primary class. Wesley and Tina, her son and daughter, five and six, sat beside her during services and never made any noise. A couple of times they had sat at the front with their father.

How could the bishop possibly want more than one wife when he had her? I couldn't imagine, for that matter, how anyone besides Sister Simpson would want the bishop for a husband. For starters, he was chubby and homely, not lean and handsome. Bald patches showed through his thinning hair. I was sure that he must have been handsome when he was younger or Sister Simpson wouldn't have married him.

Before the polygamists' visits, every Sunday morning before Sunday school Bishop Simpson stood just inside the chapel door. When I walked up the steps he smiled. "Not so fast there, young lady. You're not going to get away without a handshake from me. You make getting up in the morning worthwhile." I always laughed. I knew he was joking but he still made me feel special.

Now when he came out to church, Bishop Simpson sat with

the congregation rather than at the front. Brother Jarvis and Dad led all the meetings. I watched him. I heard the creak of weight shift on the pews as others did too. He didn't smile or even appear to notice and he was always alone.

Mom and Dad never said anything about the bishop or why he wasn't sitting at the front anymore. Rob was the only one who would answer any of my questions. "Why is Bishop Simpson sitting with the congregation?" I asked him after school one day. I purposely waited until he had finished chopping wood and taken the steps, two at a time, to his room to start on his homework. He liked any excuse to put off schoolwork.

"Dad said the bishop is having a crisis of faith over polygamy. You know Joseph Smith introduced it, right? And that the church leaders suspended it?" I nodded. Rob's eyes held my gaze as he flicked the end of his pen up and down on one of his exercise books. "The elders are giving him time to think it over. He can't carry on as a bishop, of course, but his membership is on the line. It doesn't look good."

"What do you mean, it doesn't look good?"

"If he decides to go with Joseph Smith's teachings on polygamy, the elders will kick him out of the church." I sucked in my breath. He couldn't leave. Where would he go? I wanted everything to go back to the way it had been.

When it came to polygamy, was Dad right? Was the bishop right? Was any of it right? Joseph Smith had always been a part of my life and a part of our family, from the first story Mom ever told me about him. I didn't, however, have a burning testimony inside my chest about God appearing to him. I didn't believe that God had appeared to the leaders of the church who followed after him or to the president of the church today. I could never say that out loud. I couldn't tell Mom because she would tattle on me to Dad. I had to keep pretending and keep my mouth shut. Mom and Dad's world was the church and nothing else. It didn't matter that so much didn't make sense to me. They believed it.

I was angry that the women in the church were expected to

serve their husbands as the priesthood holders and heads of the house. Even though Mom stayed home, some church women worked at jobs *and* did all the work in the house *and* took care of the children while their husbands were at church meetings. I was supposed to accept my place in the church, without question, as they did, but it didn't seem fair or right. I didn't agree with it. The women and the children were the ones that suffered.

Even though Sarah had assured me there was no danger of Dad taking up polygamy, I still woke some nights with my heart pounding. I had the same dream each time. Sarah, in the long white dress, stood beside the old man from Bountiful. Janice and I watched from a distance, and we, too, wore the same kind of dress. Once I was awake, the image of the pregnant young wife with the blank face, while her husband tried to flirt with Sarah, fixed itself firmly in my mind and wouldn't let me go back to sleep.

At church meetings, I scanned the congregation to make sure all the teenage girls were still there. Then, to be sure, I checked if any of the families were missing. Sister Simpson, Wesley, and Tina were the only ones who were gone. After Madeline told me about babysitting for Sister Simpson, I talked to Rob again. I carefully picked my time. Before supper. As soon as he went to his room to do his homework. "You can't say anything to anybody about what I tell you about the bishop, promise? You could get me into trouble." Rob nervously smoothed the wave in his black hair and held my eyes with his.

"I won't say anything to anyone. You can trust me." I instinctively placed my hand over my heart.

"The elders in the ward are having a meeting with him. He can't stay a member if he doesn't repent. Dad said Bishop Simpson is wrestling with the devil and the devil is winning. President Woods talked to him."

"No" slipped out of my mouth. The stake president wielded the power of God over the members.

"The meeting is a church court, a trial. If the bishop doesn't say he was wrong to consider polygamy and beg for forgiveness, he'll be excommunicated from the church."

I had trouble breathing. Everyone smiled and appeared happy and loving at church. Underneath the smiles lurked an unseen force, a wild animal, crouched, ready to pounce. Anyone who questioned the leaders or who didn't agree with their latest revelations would be torn apart and cast out.

The following Sunday, Bishop Simpson wasn't at Sunday school. I kept my eyes on the doors at the back of the chapel, waiting for him to walk in. When he didn't, a lump rose in my throat. I hoped that maybe he was just late. I wanted him to still be the bishop, to be at church ahead of me to shake my hand, to laugh, and to makes jokes that made me feel special. And I wanted Sister Simpson to be waiting inside the chapel for him with Wesley and Tina.

He never came through the doors. Not that week or any week after.

The Eyes of the Church

MOM BARELY GLANCED up at Janice and me as we walked into the kitchen after school. Rob and Sarah, who had gotten home first, were captivated by what she was saying, and the looks on their faces told me that something was up. Mom was still wearing her Sunday dress, and her Relief Society manual and handbag were on the table in front of her. She had unbuttoned her coat but hadn't taken it off. I plopped my schoolbooks on the table and sat down across from her.

"Can you believe it? Sister McGowan had no idea that her husband was a homosexual. After having two boys with him. You would think she'd have noticed *something*. How she's going to manage on her own, I can't imagine." Mom's voice quivered. Sister McGowan was the first friend she had made after we moved to Richmond. She was a bit odd, a nonstop talker, and Mom was on the phone with her all the time. It was as if, after living away from a church congregation for so many years, Mom was starved for a soul mate and anyone would do.

Eighteen-year-old Rob lounged against the counter with his legs stretched out. Sarah pushed past him to the sink and filled a glass with water. Mom had been visiting-teaching for the church with Sister Lucas earlier in the afternoon. They were members of the women's Relief Society, the organization that met Thursday mornings in the building beside the chapel. The women had lessons on church doctrine, on being Mormon wives and homemakers, and on storing enough food for their families to last a year. The church wanted its members to be self-sufficient in case of a natural disaster or unemployment. Food storage was based on the fear of disasters that hadn't happened but might happen.

The women's Relief Society was originally started by Joseph Smith to monitor the secret sexual practices in the church. Some of the women needed encouragement to accept and participate in the principle of plural marriage, particularly the young, unmarried girls. Those who were reluctant to accept the principle, as was Joseph's first wife Emma, were threatened with eternal damnation if they didn't. Joseph Smith married all of the members of the society, except for one, who gave him her seventeen-year-old daughter in her place.

Once a month on a weekday, Mom and Sister Lucas dressed in their Sunday clothes and visited four of the women in the ward. They gave each woman a ten-minute lesson from the church manual Salt Lake City sent out. While they were in each home, they asked the women about their families and reported their findings to Sister Baxter. She passed on the information to the bishop.

The visiting-teacher program was the counterpart of the priesthood home-teaching program. Home teachers were two priesthood holders who visited families once a month in the evening and reported back to the bishop.

"Apparently," Mom went on, "the boyfriend came for the weekend and her husband slept with him in the guest room. She told us she heard strange noises from behind the closed door." I shivered at the creepiness of it. Why had Sister McGowan stayed quiet? That part was just plain weird, although her husband not sleeping with her was also weird. Why hadn't she knocked on the door or called out to her husband and asked what was going on? At the time, I had only a vague idea of what a homosexual was. I was aware that it was a man who wanted to be with a man sexually instead of a woman. In the eyes of the church, it was a sin.

Sister McGowan, a big woman with a loud voice and thick eyeglasses, was a convert to the church. Her boys Robert and Mitchell, three and four, spat at each other and threw tantrums in the chapel. When she chased them down the aisle to the back door, her breasts jiggled underneath her sweater and her face got red.

Her husband wasn't a member of the church. If he had been, he would have been followed by priesthood holders in the ward until they caught him in a compromising position with his boyfriend. When they had evidence of his wrongdoing, the priesthood holders would have held a trial and kicked him out of the church.

I'd eavesdropped on Mom talking to Rob about Bishop Simpson's excommunication. Members who were kicked out of the church but still wanted to come to services could do so, but they weren't allowed to give talks, teach classes, or hold any church positions. They couldn't, of course, go to the celestial kingdom: the only way into that kingdom was through the temple, and they wouldn't be eligible for a temple recommend. I was certain, however, that the church would still welcome their money.

There was, however, a faint hope for redemption. If the person repented, begged for forgiveness from the bishop, and met with him regularly, they might be allowed to prove themselves worthy to be baptized a member again. Even if they were allowed back in, I couldn't imagine that anything in the church would ever be the same for them again. Wherever they moved, their church records would follow them.

Although her husband didn't fall under the jurisdiction of the church and couldn't be excommunicated, Sister McGowan did. The priesthood members would now watch her. I didn't agree with that. She didn't have a job, she might have to go on welfare, and she had two nasty little boys to take care of on her own.

Up until her visit to Sister McGowan, Mom's monthly visits had been predictable. All she usually had to talk about afterward was how clean the women kept their homes—or didn't keep them. In particular was the Sanders family, who had four children under six years old. Mom loved to tell us about them. It was the same every month. "There were dirty dishes all over the kitchen, even in the living room. Sister Sanders was still in her housecoat. And she knew we were coming." Mom always got dressed first thing in the morning. Dad didn't like to see her in her housecoat; he thought it was slovenly.

133

After one of her visits to Sister Sanders, Mom told us, "I saw a pair of underwear on the floor through her open bedroom door. I'm sure they weren't clean ones, either." As if the underwear wasn't bad enough, Mom went on: "She lets her kids eat bread and jam while they sit on the chesterfield and watch cartoons all day. They get jam all over their faces and on the upholstery and she doesn't bother to wipe them, or the furniture, off."

Mom was sure to pass the information on to Sister Baxter, who would then pass it on to Bishop Jarvis, who had replaced Bishop Simpson. What would the bishop and his counselors make of Sister Sanders's slovenliness? Dad was now first counselor. I knew what he'd think. Did the bishopric keep notes on the members? When Brother and Sister Sanders wanted to go to the temple and were interviewed for their recommend, would the bishop talk to her about her housekeeping?

Even though Dad was in the bishopric, our family wasn't exempt from the eyes of the church. Two Relief Society women visited Mom once a month while we were at school. She made sure Sarah, Janice, and I cleaned the house the day before their scheduled appointment. There wasn't anything we could do about the tattered wallpaper in the living room or the patches of linoleum on the floor. The days that they visited, I noticed at breakfast that Mom wore her favorite housedress with a fresh apron, and her hair was pulled back on one side with a barrette.

Dad wasn't involved with Mom's Relief Society activities. At suppertime, though, on the days she went out with Sister Lucas, he listened to her stories about her families. I'd heard all the stories earlier after school. The month after she told us about Sister McGowan's husband, Mom told Dad at supper one night, "Her husband has moved into Vancouver and they're going to sell the house. She'll find a place here to rent."

"That's a shame she has to sell the house." Dad lifted his fork. "Paying rent is just money down the drain. And those boys, she lets them run roughshod over her." He shook his head and started eating.

A few months later, Mom told him at supper that Sister Mc-Gowan had answered an ad in the personal column of the *Sun*. Dad stopped eating and put his fork down on his plate. "She did what?" He scowled at Mom across the table.

"I just told you, Clarence. You never listen to me. She's taking the bus up to Bella Coola to meet the man who placed the ad. He's a logger. I talked to her on the phone today."

"What about the boys?"

"It's not for a couple of weeks. She'll find someone here to babysit them. She thinks a smaller, quieter place might be good for them."

Dad's eyes narrowed. "She's not even divorced yet."

"I know, Clarence, I know. I tried to talk to her about it but she wouldn't listen to me."

After school the following week, Mom was on the phone when I came in. I knew right away who she was talking to. She stood rather than sat as she usually did and paced with the phone in her hands as far as the cord would reach. "Yes, Vivian, I can imagine you're angry. What? No, no, I had no idea the bishopric would send your home teachers over to ask about your plans to go to Bella Coola. They asked you not to give your talk at sacrament meeting? They're only trying to do what they think is right." Mom's voice was apologetic, ingratiating. Did Sister McGowan suspect Mom was lying to her and that it was Mom who had ratted her out?

After the visit from her home teachers, Sister McGowan was so angry she wrote to Salt Lake City and asked to have her name removed from the church membership records. She was one step ahead of the church. She quit before the church could hold a trial and excommunicate her.

She still took the bus up to Bella Coola. The visit with the logger didn't pan out. She never came out with her boys to church again. Mom still talked to her on the phone, but over the next few months the frequency of their calls dwindled and then stopped.

Pornography

"DAD'S HOME," I called to Mom as the bridge onto our driveway rumbled under the weight of the pickup. Dad had a job at the Terra Nova landfill in Burnaby, an hour's drive from home.

With Rob and Sarah gone, Mom had only Janice and me to help her. We each had our own bedroom, but a bedroom of my own couldn't replace Rob and Sarah. Rob was in Texas on a mission for the church. He had planned to go back to Gibsons as soon as he graduated from Richmond High, until he had a motorcycle accident. He lay in a ditch close to home with a broken leg for half a day. Drifting in and out of consciousness, he promised God that if he lived he would commit his life to the church. He accepted the call to serve as a missionary even though he still wanted to go back to Gibsons.

Mom and Dad basked in the limelight of Rob's mission. They took pride in being parents who had raised a son to serve the Lord. It increased their status in the ward in addition to Dad being in the bishopric. A mission is expected of every young priesthood holder when he turns nineteen. It is a rite of passage, essential to establishing credibility and a place in the pecking order of the church hierarchy.

I hovered close to Rob before he left, not wanting to let him out of my sight, and watched him sort his belongings into piles on his bed. "I've got something for you." He held up his cardigan from Elphinstone High in Gibsons. "I won't be needing my school sweater anymore."

The cardigan was black with two yellow bands around the left arm and buttons down the front. It hung to my knees. I wore it to

137

school every day, one way of keeping Rob with me even though he was gone.

Mom and Dad weren't as happy about Sarah leaving home. As soon as she had her secretarial certificate, she broke up with Rick instead of marrying him and moved to Calgary to work and live with church girlfriends. Mom tattled to Dad about her breaking her engagement. Rick had joined the church to please them. Dad went from disapproving of him to welcoming him into the family. I wished that Sarah had kept her breakup a secret until she was out of Dad's reach.

When Dad found out, he ambushed her in the kitchen after supper. "I hear you think you're too good for Rick now," he sneered. I backed out of the kitchen. I hurt just listening. "It's the best offer you'll get. Now that he's a Mormon, you'll have a good life. Call him and tell him you've changed your mind."

I heard Sarah say, "Dad, all I've ever done is housework, I need some freedom," before I closed my door on their voices. The next day as she packed for the bus to Calgary, her face was puffy from crying the night before. "I can't do it, I can't marry Rick," she told me. "I'm not ready to be a dairy farmer's wife. I've never had any fun." I understood why she wasn't ready to get married.

When I heard Dad's truck in the driveway, I finished changing two-month-old Peter's diaper. He lay dry and quiet in his basinet by the bay windows in the living room. I brushed my lips against his cheek, inhaled his baby-powder freshness, and reached for his soother. Michael and Ian's voices, noisy a moment before in the kitchen, faded as they rushed out the back door. It slammed with a bang that shook the floor all the way down the hall to where I stood.

What would Dad have in the back of the truck tonight? Cartons filled with bags of stale potato chips? Boxes of new shoes from the Army and Navy store in Vancouver? Plastic bags stuffed with old clothes that reeked of smoke? Maybe, just maybe, it would be some kind of food still fresh enough to eat.

Dad's arrival home at the end of a workday was just about as exciting as getting Christmas hampers from the school nurse or scavenging cull potatoes, cauliflower, and cabbage left to rot in the fields around our house. My anticipation over the food Dad brought home from the garbage dump wasn't something I shared outside the family. I didn't want anyone to know that we ate what other people threw away and wore their clothes too. What if someone recognized the clothes I was wearing as having once belonged to them?

There were some things it was okay to talk about in public and some things it wasn't. Discerning which was which had become a reflex; secrets were a normal part of being Mormon. Following the code of silence surrounding the priesthood and ceremonies in the temple, I stayed quiet about what went on at home and about the garbage we ate. Church members and the kids at school didn't eat food picked up by a garbage truck and dumped at a landfill to be buried under mountains of dirt.

At school, I stared with longing at what the kids tossed into the metal waste basket: half-eaten sandwiches and apples with only a bite or two out of them. Even though my stomach was hollow, I couldn't ask them to give me what they were throwing out. To say the truth, that I was hungry, would set me farther apart and make them pity me more than they already did. Every time the group of popular girls in my homeroom class pointedly noticed the clothes I was wearing and whispered to each other, I wanted to go home.

Eating the food Dad brought from the garbage dump was different. I didn't see who had thrown it away and they didn't see me eating it. Because I was hungry, I was thankful for everything Dad scavenged, yet I was ashamed at the same time. Grateful anticipation battled with embarrassment. There was so much in my life I didn't talk about.

President Woods had gotten Dad the job at the landfill. He was the developer who had arranged for the sale of the property for Terra Nova. His friendship with Dad had developed at the meetings in Vancouver for the bishoprics in the Lower Mainland.

On the afternoon Mom drove Janice, the boys, and me to

watch Dad on the bulldozer at his new job, we stayed in the station wagon with the windows rolled up. Landfill was a euphemism for the dump. I held my nose and kept my mouth closed against the stench of rotting waste that seeped into my very pores. Dad sat high above the ground on the seat of the D8, a conquering beast that roared as it chewed up piles of stinking garbage and covered them with dirt. Seagulls cawed and careened in circles around his head. Back at home, I heated water in the canner on the woodstove and had a bath to get the smell off.

After his first week at the landfill, at the supper table on Friday night, Dad said, "It's not such a bad job." He lifted his spoon and paused with it in mid-air. We were eating hot stewed tomatoes. He had brought home a case of overripe ones the night before. Mom had cut off the bad bits, a messy job that stained her hands and apron, and cooked them up. We stirred in cubes of bread that softened into a mush as they soaked up the juice. Seasoned with salt it was delicious.

"It took me a few days to get used to the smell. The first day it made me kind of sick but I don't even notice it anymore. It's honest work. A fellow could do worse things for a regular paycheck."

Since we moved to Richmond, Dad had earned money building houses and doing renovations. He'd bought and sold logging equipment and horses and raised calves as beef cattle. He'd gone commercial fishing for one season on a boat out of Steveston and worked at a forge in a rundown industrial area called Granville Island. He grew Blue Lake pole beans on our property for two summers. We kids and Mom weeded and picked the beans and Dad trucked them to the cannery. I didn't mind working on the beans, although Dad said the earnings were dismal.

"There's a trick to working at the dump," Dad said the night we ate Mom's tomato dish. "I'm starting to get the hang of it." He leaned back in his chair and reached for a toothpick from the cut-glass container in the middle of the table. "What counts is joking around and getting on good terms with the drivers who come in with their loads. The dairy and the bakery guys have started to leave their good stuff for me by the shed. If the bigger trucks have something worth any money, say copper wire or metals, they'll dump it by the side of the shed, too. There's a lot of money to be made in that alone." Over the next few months, with the help of Michael and Ian, Dad built a barrier behind the house to keep all the extras he brought home out of sight.

One Sunday when the missionaries were invited for dinner, after we finished eating Dad bragged about his skill driving the bulldozer. "The RCMP often bring in confiscated cases of liquor or stolen electronic equipment. They won't leave until they've seen me bury it. I slowly give it a light cover of dirt while they watch, being careful not to crush the goods. Then, after they leave, I take a run at it from the other direction, dig the blade in deep, and roll it out." Dad leaned back in his chair and rested his forearms on the table. "The liquor's no use to me, of course, but the drivers who come in are happy to get it."

The nineteen-year-old missionaries smiled and nodded as if they were impressed, as if they thought Dad was amazingly talented. I believed he was myself. What did the missionaries really think? Did they think Dad was being dishonest and were too polite to tell him?

It was Mom, not Dad, who told Janice and me about the magazines the drivers dropped off at the shed that was used for an office. I had just pegged the clothes out on the clothesline, one of my after-school chores, and come into the kitchen with the empty basket. Janice was at the counter peeling potatoes.

"It's amazing what comes into the dump," Mom said as she bent and punched down dough in the bread pan. "Dad says stacks of girlie magazines are left all the time." My eyes met Janice's. I had seen adult magazines they didn't sell to minors, half-hidden behind the counter at the convenience store in Brighouse. Mom lifted the bread dough a few inches, sprinkled it with flour, and plopped it back down in the pan. "Dad thought I should be aware of what's going on in the world. He brings them home for us to read." She stood up and shifted her shoulders.

Why was she telling us about the magazines? I had the urge to gag, the way I did when she left the bathroom door wide open when she went in to use the toilet. I had never noticed Dad bringing in any magazines from work. How did he sneak them into the house? I didn't want to know. "Some of the pictures are quite unbelievable." Mom's lips curved in a little smile and her eyes widened. She shook her head, then bent back down over the dough.

The thought of Mom and Dad poring over pictures of naked men and women behind their bedroom door, and Mom telling us about it, made me nauseated. I couldn't imagine either of them confessing to Bishop Jarvis when they had their temple recommends renewed that they read girlie magazines. There is a list of questions about sexual purity that the bishop asks each member during the interview. With Dad being one of his counselors, the bishop probably wouldn't imagine it was a question he needed to ask.

Even though Dad had a regular paycheck and earned extra money from scavenging at the landfill, Janice still cleaned a woman's house after school. I still bought my own shoes and personal items from babysitting money and wore Janice's hand-me-downs and clothes from the dump. I was learning to sew in home economics class. Michael still fell asleep with his head on his desk at school, exhausted from his morning and after-school paper routes and the work he did for Dad at home. Nothing had changed.

One afternoon in the spring as I walked home from the bus stop, I thought about how we were no further ahead. I seethed at having to pay tithing. At home, I dropped my books on the kitchen table and complained bitterly to Mom. "Why do we have to pay tithing on the money we earn? I wish I didn't have to." She stopped chopping vegetables, her expression solemn, without words.

I wanted to wear brand new clothes like my classmates at school. Owning a record player of my own was out of the question, as was the holiday at a dude ranch that some of the girls were going on during summer holidays. I would be babysitting and picking berries to earn money for school supplies next year. When I was twelve, before Sarah left home, Mom had tried to get me work as a live-in nanny during the summer. The one awkward interview she took me on stalled when the woman told Mom she thought I was much too young to be living and working away from home. I thought at the time that Mom wanted me, and all my questions about the church, out of the way.

"Paying tithing is a privilege, a way to contribute to spreading the gospel," Mom finally said. "It's why we've been sent here to earth. We're helping Rob on his mission, and it's really not costing us anything because we save so much money by being members of the church. The money we don't spend on cigarettes and alcohol we send to Rob."

Resentment smoldered inside me, like the underground fire that smoked just below the surface of Terra Nova in hot weather: unseen, yet dangerous. Mom and Dad gave their money to the church while I wore clothes people threw out and ate vegetables left to rot and food from a garbage dump.

Free Agency?

I SLOUCHED ON a chair in the back row of Brother Adderson's Sunday school class and filed my nails. I knew it was rude. I half-expected him to get mad at me and was surprised when he didn't. If he noticed, he pretended not to. An image of the ocean and the sound of the tide rushing over the sand rescued me from the monotony of his voice talking about church doctrine. Those Gibsons pleasures were gone forever. Their loss was an ever-present weight that kept my spirit small and subdued. With Rob and Sarah gone, there was no one at home to dull the sting. Sitting on a metal chair in Brother Adderson's class in a basement room with no windows was the last place most fourteen-year-old girls, especially me, wanted to be. The choice wasn't mine to make. I was a marionette, with Mom and Dad pulling the strings.

Every Sunday morning after Dad left for church, I protested to Mom, "I don't want to go to church anymore. Why can't I stay home? What about the free agency I'm supposed to have?"

"Free agency" is a basic tenet of the church. Supposedly, it means that every person is free to choose between good or evil. In practice, however, choosing good translated into obeying church authority and Mom and Dad. Thinking for myself, questioning church practices, and making decisions about my own spiritual practice translated into choosing evil. In theory, I could choose my own path, but if my own path didn't follow all the church rules, it would be the wrong choice.

I tried to reason with Mom on Sunday mornings. No matter what tack I tried or what argument I put forth, her eyes glazed over and she got annoyed. Her answer was always the same: "That's Sa-

145

tan talking to you. Why are you such a troublemaker? Why can't you just do as you're told? I've got enough on my plate with the boys and the new baby." She was worn out since she had Peter, and while I didn't want to add to her weariness, the voice inside me refused to stay silent.

Every weekday morning while it was still dark and cold, I was forced awake at five-thirty to go to an hour-long class on church doctrine, called Seminary, before regular school started. Janice went willingly. My body was present while my mind ran free and my eyes watched the clock.

In Brother Adderson's Sunday school class, I checked my cuticles. I had heard there was a kit at the drugstore to help shape them. The article in *Seventeen Magazine* that I had read at the school library said that manicured nails were a must for every young woman, a sign of good grooming. I wanted to be noticed by a boy two grades ahead of me at school. I had tried coloring my hair with red food dye, but it only stained my fingers and neck and the towels I used. I was too scared to try anything stronger. Mom didn't say anything about the red food coloring I had bought with my babysitting money. Janice rolled her eyes. Michael and Ian laughed at me and told people at church. I cringed with embarrassment at that.

When Brother Adderson began to talk about a summer job he had as a teenager in Saskatchewan, I noticed the change in his voice and came back to the room. I looked at him, really looked at him: tall and lean, middle-aged, his red hair thinning, his face covered in summer freckles. His tie was rumpled and off-center, caught under the left lapel of his suit jacket as if he had rushed to get dressed. I imagined he had been handsome when he was younger.

I had missed the part about why he was telling us the story. He'd had a crush on a Mennonite girl whose family owned the fields he worked in. She and her brothers watched over the workers from a small shack on one side of the field. At the end of each workday, he lingered beside the shack and made excuses to talk to her. Afterward, his heart pounding, he got on his bicycle and pedaled home. At night he dreamed about her.

On the last day of work before he went back to school, he persuaded her to stay after her brothers had left for home. All eleven of us in the class, even the boys, leaned forward on our chairs. He had my full attention now. "She was beautiful," he said. "Liquid brown eyes that made me quiver all over. Small white teeth. Clear pink skin." A boyish expression softened his face. "I didn't care that she was a Mennonite and I was a Mormon. I was in love." My metal chair scratched on the concrete floor as I shifted my weight. One of the boys cleared his throat.

"She wouldn't let me kiss her goodbye," he told us, "no matter how much I tried to talk her into it. Instead, she rolled up one of her long sleeves to just above her elbow and let me stroke her arm." He paused. His Adam's apple moved up and down as he swallowed. "It was the most exciting moment of my life." I shivered at the thought of having my arm stroked by a boy in love with me.

"At the time, all I wanted to do was kiss and cuddle her. I couldn't think of anything else. Now I'm glad she said no. I could so easily have fallen into sin if she'd let me kiss her. And where would I be today if I had?" We kids all focused on the floor. I didn't dare glance over at any one of them. I was afraid I would burst into nervous giggles.

"I was lucky. She didn't go to my school, and although I searched for her whenever I went into town, I never saw her. I didn't have to face temptation with her again. The following year, I finished high school and went on a mission. She gradually faded from my heart." I wished he'd seen her again. Was she in love with him? She must have been or she wouldn't have stayed on and let him stroke her arm.

"Can you imagine the pain I would have caused my parents if I had chased after a girl who wasn't a member of the church? I could have saved myself a lot of anguish if I'd remembered what God wanted for me, rather than being swayed by my own selfish desires."

I was sorry that Brother Adderson had fallen in love with a

Mennonite girl rather than a Mormon one. I vowed to stop filing my nails in his Sunday school class. Maybe he would tell more of his stories about growing up, instead of the boring lessons from the Sunday school manual that I never listened to. At least his stories were a little bit interesting even if they always came back around to Mormonism.

I knew for sure that the church and the lessons about doctrine weren't for me. Yet while I lived at home, I had no choice but to attend. The only choice I had was how soon I left home. Only then would I truly have the freedom to choose what I wanted. I had no idea what that was, but I needed to find out.

No More Children

"THE DOCTOR SAYS I have no choice." Mom's voice was weak. "If they don't operate, I'll bleed to death." My stomach flipped over. She was lying on the chesterfield in the living room. Her face was pale and her eyes blinked away tears. Two-year-old Peter played with his cars on the floor beside her. Janice and I had just come home from school.

"They're going to take my uterus out to stop the bleeding. It's called a hysterectomy. Dr. Matthews has arranged for an emergency operation tomorrow at Grace Hospital." A sick sensation lodged in my chest. Mom's spirit was draining away with her blood. I didn't want to think of her body being cut into and a part of her taken out. What if she died? I wished I could stretch my hands out and have healing power from God flow through me into Mom, as Jesus did in the Bible. Only men were supposed to do the healing in the church, using the power of the priesthood passed down from Joseph Smith. I had never known of anyone being miraculously healed by the priesthood.

Bitterness burned my insides. It was the church's fault that Mom needed the operation. Mormon women were expected to have as many children as they could. It was one of the outward signs of their devoutness. The only time Dad gave Mom flowers, at least that I knew of, was when she had a baby. I counted up the number of times she had been pregnant: eight living babies, two miscarriages, and a dead baby. The dead baby died inside her at six months after she fell through a rotted clothesline platform before our move to the little house around the bay in Gibsons. She carried the baby for the next three months until Dad could afford to take

149

her into the hospital in Vancouver.

"My body just never recovered from lifting all those heavy chicken crates on the farm years ago," Mom said. "That was when your dad was away at a lumber camp."

I clamped my mouth shut and gritted my teeth so hard my jaw hurt. She blamed Dad being away and the work she did while he was gone, rather than the number of her pregnancies. I believed that her body had simply worn out from pregnancy and childbirth. I didn't dare tell her that, no matter how much I wanted to. Janice, standing beside me, didn't say anything either. I didn't know what she thought—ever. She never shared her thoughts. I had given up trying to talk to her about anything that was important to me or expecting her to confide in me. Most of the time she acted as if I was beneath her, and she was sarcastic in the way that Dad was to Mom and Sarah. She behaved just like him.

"Sister Phillips will take care of Peter during the day when I'm in the hospital." Mom eyes met mine. "I'll need you to take care of me and Peter when I get home. I won't be able to lift anything." I groaned inwardly. I would miss my friends at school and be behind everyone in my classes. It wasn't as if I had a choice though. There was no one else.

Mom never kept Janice home: her grades were too important. She had taken grade seven and eight in one year. She was going to university. I had stopped expecting, or asking, to have the same things as she had. It hurt too much when I didn't get them. Mom and Dad paid for music lessons for Janice and for painting and craft lessons, even though she wasn't musical or creative. I taught myself how to play the piano from her discarded music books after she gave up. The sandals I crafted from cardboard shredded apart the first time I wore them. Only the rag straps tied to my feet were left. Using cardboard, all I had, was a mistake.

The first time Mom kept me home from school, I was in grade one. "God's law is higher than any laws man can make about going to school," she told me. "I need you at home to help." I knew better than to protest. If I did, she would tell Dad on me. The thought of what he'd do to me kept me quiet and compliant. When it came right down to it though, if Mom needed my help, I wanted to do everything I could. I was tied to her, and always had been, as if we were in a three-legged race together.

That evening, while she got ready to go to the hospital, I stayed close to her. I stood in her bedroom while she laid her housecoat on the bed beside a small suitcase and reached for the brush on her dresser. "There'll be no more babies in our family." Her voice was heavy with sorrow. I was sorry about how unhappy she was and worried for her too. At the same time I was relieved.

Mom was in the hospital for ten days. Partway through her stay, Dad drove us all over to visit her after he came home from work. Children under sixteen weren't allowed inside. We stood beside the station wagon in the parking lot, gazed up at her face in the open window on the third floor, and waved. I could barely make out her face. I knew from her black hair and the way she tilted her head that it was Mom.

Janice and I played hopscotch with Michael and Ian on the asphalt while Dad was inside. We took turns holding Peter's hand whenever a car drove in or out of the parking lot. Dad came out the front doors with a paper bag filled with cellophane-wrapped crackers and cookies that Mom had saved from her food trays. I was excited. We never had these kinds of treats at home.

The house was empty without Mom. I counted the days until she would be home. Sister Watson, the new president of the Relief Society, arranged for members to bring over bread they had baked and containers of stew and casseroles. The day before Mom came home, Janice and I made the boys put their toys away. We washed clothes, swept the floors, did all the dishes, and scrubbed off the kitchen counters.

Mom leaned on Dad's arm as she came in the back kitchen door. At the sight of her wan face and wobbly fragility, I went woozy myself. "I'm so happy to be home again." Wincing in pain, she lowered herself into the bed Janice and I had made on the chesterfield in the living room so she could be close to the bathroom. Dad drove to the drugstore to get her a prescription.

That evening, we tiptoed around while Mom slept. In the morning before Dad left for work, he stoked up the fires in the fireplace and the woodstove in the kitchen. The spring weather was still cool. When the fires burned down, the house quickly became damp and chilled.

The first day that Mom was home, I kept watch over her from the doorway of the living room. Her eyelashes fluttered against her pale face while she dozed. Every time the covers over her chest moved up and down, the tight coil of anxiety inside me unwound a half turn. I was thankful she was still breathing. Peter tried to push past my legs to get to her, but I kept a tight grip on his arm. "Mom needs to sleep and you'll hurt her if you crawl up on her," I whispered in his ear. He didn't understand, or if he did he still wanted to get to her. I glanced at the clock. After I fed him a peanut butter sandwich for lunch, he could go down for an afternoon nap.

On my first day back at school, Mom sent a note: *Maggie was needed at home.* Mrs. Neilson, the secretary in the office, smiled at me across the counter. As she read Mom's writing, her face softened. "Everything okay at home now?" she asked. I nodded, a lump in my throat at her kindness. My face was hot as I backed out the office door and scurried down the hall to my locker.

There was no one I could talk to about Mom's hysterectomy or about my feelings at being kept home from school. I was envious of the kids who weren't members of the church, who came from small families, and who didn't have to stay away from school to help out at home. Those kids lived in a world I could never be part of.

My emotions tumbled and festered as I mulled over what the church's teachings did to women's bodies. It finally occurred to me that Mom was free at last. The hysterectomy was a blessing. She would never be pregnant again. Her suffering was over.

Mine had just begun. The thought of having to go through what Mom had gone through tormented me. I didn't want to follow the teachings of the church. I didn't want my body used up by childbearing. Mom and Dad expected me to do as I was told and obediently accept my preordained role as a woman in the church. The last thing I wanted was a life like Mom's.

Butter and Bread

THE LAMPLIGHT CAST a halo on the wood paneling in Donna's rec room. The August heat inside was stifling. Paul Anka's voice crooned from the record player on the table beside the closed door, "Put your head on my shoulder . . ."

My heart pumped in double time as Lynden Billings and I, our bodies pressed together, arms draped around each other, swayed in time to the music. Lynden was fifteen, my age, and was from England. On probation for stealing a car and driving around Burnaby with his friends, he lived at Brother and Sister Kenwood's house in our ward even though he wasn't a Mormon. They had an extra bedroom and did foster care to earn money. My cheek nestled in the crook of Lynden's shoulder and the warm skin-scent of his neck poured through me. I kept my eyes closed and pretended that the other four couples weren't here.

"You're sure your mom won't come down?" I heard Mike, Donna's boyfriend, ask over the music. "Maybe we should turn all the lights back on."

"She's watching Ben Casey. I'll go upstairs and get more chips and dip. She'll never come down." Donna and Mike had met at the Seminary class we all went to in Vancouver before school started each morning. Donna, her older sister Kim, and her mom were converts to the church. Her mom was divorced. They lived in a rented house with tired paint and a scraggly lawn, on Number Two Road close to the church and a couple of miles from where we lived. They had moved into the ward the year before. After their first time at Sunday school, Mom said on our drive home, "They don't have the best background, with no father around, but they're part of our church family now."

Donna's party was the first private one I had been invited to. I had never been included in any of the parties the kids at my school had. The parties I went to were teenage socials in the building next to the chapel in Richmond or in the gym at the Vancouver ward on 41st Avenue. The church had teenage potluck dinners and picnics, car washes to raise money for the building fund, swimming and skating outings, and dances for everyone over fourteen. Sometimes we went to Walt Disney movies, the only movies that the church approved of.

When the song finished, Lynden guided me over to one of the easy chairs and eased me down onto his lap. I held onto him, dizzy with pleasure. His bony knees jabbed into the back of my thighs. He pulled me against him and moved his mouth against mine. My first kiss. At the movie theater, whenever two people came together in a kiss on screen, like Elvis Presley in *Blue Hawaii*, a movie I'd snuck off to, I was breathless, faint. Goosebumps rose on my arms. I didn't feel breathless when Lynden kissed me; all I felt was his wet mouth tasting of chip dip. His body rubbing against mine while we were pseudo-dancing had been more exciting.

Lynden, skinny and short-haired with a snub nose, wasn't what you'd call handsome. When he came out to church with the Kenwoods, his English accent had been a magnet. Brother Kenwood introduced him to Allen, Sandy, Madeline, and me, who were all in the same Sunday school class. We stood in a group on the grass in the warm June sunshine outside the chapel doors, waiting until the last minute to go inside.

Even before I heard Lynden's voice, I knew he was different. He wasn't wearing a suit, just dress pants and a white shirt. A muscle twitched in his cheek. He shifted from foot to foot and kept his hands in his pockets. Plump, red-haired Allen shook his hand and said, "Nice to meet you, man." I nodded and smiled and wished that I was pretty. Sandy ran her fingers through her hair and Madeline giggled. After the introductions, Allen carried on talking about his summer plans. I wanted him to stop talking so I could hear

Lynden's voice again. "What are you going to do for the summer?" Allen finally asked him.

"Dunno wot yet." Lynden shifted his weight and kicked at the grass. "I'm going ter change the oil in Mr. Kenwood's Volvo next week. I want to be a mechanic, yeah. 'E's going to help me get into a course."

"I love cars too," I jumped in. "I used to help my brother Rob work on our station wagon all the time. What kind of motor oil are you going to use?" I lied about helping Rob. I knew nothing about cars.

"Dunno. Depends on wot Mr. Kenwood wants to use, yeah."

In the following weeks, I quivered with excitement before services because I knew Lynden would be there. As soon as Sunday school or sacrament meeting let out, Lynden was out the door. He waited for Brother Kenwood on the front lawn where everyone mingled and chatted. He slouched with his hands in his pockets and listened to Allen talk. I sidled over to join them, trying to make it appear as if I had just naturally landed beside them.

The afternoon of Donna's party I tried on all my clothes in various combinations, and came up with four possibilities. I decided to wear Sarah's hand-me-down pink pencil skirt, a white blouse, and a thick black belt. The skirt was a bit snug. I checked to make sure the bumps of my garters didn't show.

Mom drove me to the party. "I'll pick you up at ten o'clock. Have a good time and remember who you are." My stomach recoiled. Did she always have to spoil everything? She was talking about being a Mormon. Her words were a suffocating cage, so small I could barely move inside it. I half-expected her to start humming, "I am a child of God, And he has sent me here, Has given me an earthly home with parents kind and dear . . ."

I watched the station wagon drive away and immediately felt lighter. A tiny part of me wanted to please Mom, to be the good Mormon she wanted me to be in exchange for her love and approval. Most of me was desperate to escape from her and Dad and the church. "Remember who you are," she had said. Who was I? I had no idea. I only knew what I wasn't—everything Mom wanted me to be and the person I pretended to be, to stay safe at home from Dad.

I sat on Lynden's lap in the muggy semi-darkness, our mouths together, dreading ten o'clock and the end of my freedom. I couldn't tell Mom that I had spent the whole evening with my body glued against Lynden's or that Donna had turned off the lights so that everyone could kiss. If I ever wanted to go to another private party, I would have to make up a story about playing board games or watching TV and eating popcorn. If Mom found out that some of the kids weren't members of the church, her face would twist in disapproval. I probably wouldn't be allowed to go to another one.

Mom and Dad wanted Sarah, Janice, and me to marry Mormon boys, just as long as they weren't black. Mom would wake up with nightmares about one of us marrying a black man. They could join the church, although they weren't allowed to hold the priesthood. Joseph Smith described them as a "loathsome race." With that kind of description, why would anyone who was black ever want to join? I knew from the Bible stories Mom read when I was young that Cain and his descendants had their skin turned black as punishment after Cain killed his brother Abel.

The only black person I had ever met was my science teacher at Richmond High, Harry Jerome, a famous sprinter. As far as I was concerned, he was the same as all my white teachers except for his celebrity status. He wasn't a Mormon, but his wife, who was Caucasian, had come out to a few church events. Madeline and I babysat his daughter in the building next to the chapel.

Mormon girls often got married when they graduated from high school or as soon as their boyfriends were released from serving a mission. Mom drove Janice and me into the monthly church dances at the Vancouver ward on Saturday nights, in the hope that we would both meet Mormon boys. She drove back to pick us up at eleven o'clock. After the first dance, she asked us on the drive home, "Did you have a good time?" Her voice was tired. "Who did you dance with?"

I couldn't bear to disappoint her. "Oh, just some of the guys who were there."

"Was there anyone there that caught your attention?" Her voice was hopeful.

The truth was that I had spent most of the evening hanging out at the corner store on Oak Street with Sandy and Madeline, buying penny candy, because none of the boys had asked me to dance. I wanted boys to pay attention to me, although no boy in particular. It hadn't happened yet. "The Johnson boy was really nice," Janice said from the backseat she had to herself. "He's planning to go to the University of British Columbia too, when he graduates from high school next year. I wonder whether we'll be in any of the same classes."

There was concern in Mom's eyes as she glanced over at me. "Maybe you'll meet someone at one of the stake conferences." I didn't hold out any hope for that. Stake conference was held in Vancouver four times a year. All the members from the wards in the Lower Mainland attended. The teenagers funneled into a separate classroom for the afternoon service on Sunday. At the conference the past spring, Brother Clarke, a guest speaker from Salt Lake City, had told stories as part of his talk. He'd worn a suit similar to the rest of the men, except that his was of a higher quality. As he talked, he paced the width of the room in front of us.

"You know when you're hungry how you look forward to eating a fresh piece of bread with butter on it?" His eyes moved over us slouching on the rows of folding chairs. "The kind of bread your mothers bake. You think about how delicious that bread is and how good it's going to taste." He paused and cleared his throat. Even though I had just eaten lunch, I was suddenly hungry.

"How would you feel about that piece of bread and butter if someone had dropped the bread on the floor first and it got dirty, or if they'd licked all the butter off before they handed it to you?" He stopped pacing, took a breath, and gazed at us intently, then continued louder than before. "Not very good, I'll bet. Would you still want to eat that bread? Would you find it appealing?" Did he think we were stupid? The answer was obvious.

"Marriage," his voice continued to rise, "is a piece of buttered bread. But only if it's fresh and unspoiled. Girls." His eyes electrified. "And you girls. You are the butter on the bread of marriage. It's up to each one of you to make sure you keep yourself fresh and clean. Don't let the butter on your bread get licked off. If you do, what boy will want your hand in a temple marriage?" He shook his head as if in despair.

Everyone held their breath. I was afraid to move. Much as I wanted to, I didn't dare look around at my girlfriends behind me to gauge what they thought. Brother Clarke might notice and say something. What was Sandy thinking? What kind of bread would Brother Clarke think she was? She'd sworn me to secrecy about what had happened with Brother Buckley.

Brother Buckley was a handsome Irish cop with a wife and family. Everything about him was big: his voice, his laugh, his personality, and he joked with everyone. His black curly hair fell across his forehead, and he had blue eyes. When he smiled his face lit up and his teeth flashed.

"Call me Bucky," he'd said with a laugh when he moved into the ward. And we all did. He was the only man that we teenagers didn't call the prescribed "Brother." Sandy babysat his children most Saturday nights. The Buckleys were in the ward for two years until Bucky got a transfer to a police station in the Interior. The fun left with him.

After they moved, in one of my marathon Friday night phone conversations with Sandy, I told her how much I missed Bucky. She went quiet. "There's something I need to tell you," she finally blurted out. "You've got to promise not to say anything to anybody." It was my turn to fall silent. "I knew he liked me in a special way," she said. "He made me feel as if I was grown-up, even though I was only fourteen. He always singled me out to talk to after church while Sister Buckley got the kids into the car." I gripped the phone, hard.

"One Saturday night when he drove me home from babysitting, he stopped the car at the end of my driveway where there were no lights." She paused and took a breath. A sick sensation pulsed through me.

"He grabbed me so hard I thought I was going to throw up. His mouth smashed against mine. Even my teeth hurt. I couldn't breathe. He moaned and gasped and kept saying my name over and over. It went on forever." I hoped that she wasn't going to cry. "When he finally let go of me, my lips and face were all bruised and swollen. He didn't say a word. I staggered out of his car and snuck into the house so Mom and Daddy wouldn't see me. Thank goodness they were in bed. Daddy would have killed Bucky if he'd seen my face. He was in the forces."

I wanted more details but thought any questions might make her feel worse than she already did. Had Bucky done more than just kiss her? Was she afraid to tell me? How could he have attacked her? He was a priesthood holder with a wife and family. He and Sister Buckley went to the temple.

"After that night I avoided him at church. I couldn't bear to talk to him, even though I thought about him all the time. Each time Sister Buckley telephoned to ask me to babysit, I came up with excuses and she stopped calling. I was relieved when they moved away. Promise me you won't tell anyone."

Questions raced through my mind. What would Sandy's parents have done if she had told them about what Bucky did to her? And what would the bishop have done? Say she must have been mistaken? Blamed her? Would anything have happened to Bucky? Had he attacked any of the other church girls?

As I listened to Brother Clarke from Salt Lake, I wondered what he would have to say about what had been done to Sandy. In the eyes of the church, had Sandy had the butter licked off her? Was she now a spoiled, dirty piece of bread that no one would want to take to the temple?

Until I met Lynden a few months after Brother Clarke's talk, no one had had any interest in licking the butter off me. I had wondered what I would do if someone tried, and the thought both thrilled and terrified me. Now it had happened. When it did, I didn't even think about Brother Clarke's warnings. I didn't care that Lynden wasn't a Mormon or that as soon as his probation was over he would be gone. When I heard his voice, my heart went whoomp! I wanted him to like me as much as I liked him, even though nothing stirred inside me when he kissed me. Being with him was enough. If kissing me made him like me more, I hoped there would be another opportunity soon. He could lick all the butter off me that he wanted. I didn't plan on going to the temple.

Predator

"MAGGIE CAN GO," Dad said. I wished that I'd gone into the house as soon as we got home. If Dad hadn't seen me, maybe he'd have offered up Janice instead of me.

It was the summer I turned sixteen. Dad leaned against the back of the station wagon and talked to Brother Roy in our driveway while Mom stood off to one side. Brother Roy was a short man, big and twice as wide as Dad. He lived somewhere in Vancouver but had been invited to Richmond as a guest speaker. He was higher up in the church than Dad.

"I saw your girls in the meeting tonight and a light bulb went on. My neighbor's wife is in the hospital. The poor fellow's been left to manage for a week on his own with two little kids." He took a crumpled handkerchief from his pants pocket and mopped at the perspiration on his bald head. "It would be a big help if you could spare one of your girls to babysit. How his wife expected him to manage on his own without getting her mother over from Toronto, I can't imagine." Dad shook his head and made a tsk sound in agreement.

I didn't know Brother Roy. I didn't know his neighbor. The last thing I wanted to do was babysit two kids, clean, cook, and wash a stranger's clothes while staying overnight with him for a week. My summer was already planned. Each weekday and on Saturdays too, I was going to earn money strawberry picking in Steveston.

I didn't want to be away from home, even for a week. Besides not being able to pick berries, I would miss any letters from Don. We'd met the past Christmas at a dance in Gibsons, when I visited Christine. Don was four years older. He was living with his grand-

163

parents in Vancouver while he studied engineering at the British Columbia Institute of Technology in Burnaby. He had just flown up to Moresby Island in the Queen Charlottes to work for the summer at a logging camp. Every time I opened our mailbox and glimpsed my name in his sloping handwriting, my heart lurched.

Reading his letters, I saw him as clearly as if he were standing in front of me: slouched against his Chevy with his hands in his pockets, his blond hair combed in a wave, his smile showing a tiny chip on one of his teeth. Mom and Dad knew his parents in Gibsons, the only reason they had allowed me to go out with him.

Dad hadn't asked me if I wanted to babysit for Brother Roy's neighbor, hadn't even asked how much I would be paid. I was too afraid of Dad to ask those questions myself. A picture of me sloshing dirty work jeans in a wringer washer in a dim basement popped depressingly into my mind. I saw myself buttering bread on a stained Formica counter to make sandwiches for the man's lunch kit, while his runny-nosed children whined for me to make their porridge. Even worse, I was smiling and pretending to like them.

"I don't think it's a good idea for her to babysit if there's no woman in the house." Mom's voice was low. She stared directly at Dad. "And they're not Mormon." She brushed at the skirt of her dress as if there were crumbs on it.

"Oh it'll be fine," Dad said. "It's right next door to Brother Roy's. He'll keep an eye on her." The deferential tone he used with Brother Roy was gone when he talked to Mom. Her mouth tightened. She turned and walked into the house.

I shifted from one foot to the other on the dirt driveway, my despair deepening. I would have to go. It was unthinkable for me to stand up to Dad and say no. I was sure if I did, Dad would grab my arm, march me into the house, and yell, "How dare you embarrass me. You'll do what you're told." I didn't dare say what I wanted. It was too dangerous. I stayed mute.

That same evening Brother Roy drove me to Vancouver. The daylight faded to dusk on the drive. All the windows of his Rambler were rolled down and a hot, dry breeze blew through the car. I sat on the front seat as close to the passenger door as possible. His sweaty body odor wafted over to me in waves. I tried to breathe out rather than in.

"You must be really proud of your brother Rob for going on a mission," he said, glancing over at me. "Your Dad mentioned now that Rob's been released, he's in Los Angeles staying at your uncle's and taking a court reporting course. And engaged to marry one of the converts he baptized in Texas. Imagine that." For the rest of the half-hour drive, he talked nonstop about the missionary program for the church. I wished I was home.

He pulled over in front of a house on a dark, tree-lined street. "Here we are. My house is right next door." Doom flooded me. I got out of the car, my body heavy and sluggish. My legs were stiff and slow as I walked up the stairs beside him to the front door. I swallowed, my mouth dry. He rapped lightly.

The man who opened the door had greasy black hair, was unshaven, and wore a sleeveless undershirt. He rubbed his eyes. Curly chest hair showed above the neckline of his undershirt. My breathing slowed. Below drooping sweatpants his feet were bare. *Get me out of here.* I was stuck. Dad had sent me.

"I told you I'd find someone to help you out, didn't I? You sure were surprised when I phoned earlier." Brother Roy chuckled. He was pleased with himself. "Maggie's come all the way from Richmond. Maggie, my neighbor Mr. Carter." My heart thundered in my ears. I made my lips turn up in a smile.

"Am I happy you're here." Mr. Carter's smile was wide. His teeth were crooked.

"Maggie's used to babysitting and helping out at home, so you're in good hands. You'll be able to go to work tomorrow."

After the door closed behind Brother Roy and his footsteps creaked down the steps, I clung to my overnight bag and didn't move. A worn couch, matching chair, and scratched coffee table crowded the room. In one corner, a small television sat on top of a cabinet. I smelled fried fish sticks.

"Sit down, sit down." I moved to the chair and sat. "Call me Bill. No need to be formal. The kids are already upstairs asleep so there's just the two of us here." I trembled and barely breathed. He pushed a stack of newspapers on the chesterfield to one side and sat down across from me, leaning forward with his arms resting on his legs. "So, you go to the same church as my neighbor, eh? You're a Mormon, right? I go to the United Church. Mormons have big families. I guess you have a lot of brothers and sisters, eh?"

"Yes."

"How old are you?"

"Sixteen."

"Have you got a boyfriend?"

"Sort of." It was none of his business. I shifted in the chair, clutched the edges of the arms, and wished he would talk about something else.

"There's a lot of kids in the youth group at my church who are going out with each other. I often wonder what they get up to. So easy for them to get into trouble, if you get my meaning." His voice dropped as if he was sharing a secret. I moved as far back in the chair as I could.

"How far do you think teenagers should go with each other?" His eyes slid from my face to my breasts. A tremor started in my chest and expanded until my whole body shook.

"I don't know," I whispered, turning away and inspecting the fireplace, longing to be home, to be anywhere except here.

"I have to get up early in the morning. Do you want to sleep in my room or on the couch? If you sleep in my room, I might just wander in by mistake when I get up to go to the bathroom."

"I'll sleep on the couch."

He pulled some blankets out of the cupboard in the corner. "Oh, and if it's your funny time, you'll find something in the cabinet in the bathroom." I cringed as if he'd touched me. No one, not Mom or my sisters or my girlfriends, ever talked about their menstrual periods. They were too personal.

I heard the bedsprings squeak as Mr. Carter got into bed in his room next to the living room. I crept into the bathroom across the hall, my pajamas and housecoat clutched against my chest. Thankfully, there was a lock on the door. I changed into my pajamas as fast as I could.

I tiptoed back to the living room and crawled into the makeshift bed of blankets, dressed in my two layers of clothes. Motionless, eyes open, every nerve raw, I listened to the creak and groan of the bedsprings in the bedroom. Was that his breathing coming through the wall? Would he get up in the dark and come into the living room?

Did a half hour pass or an hour? Or was it only ten minutes before my stomach cramped in pain? I lay as still as I could, hoping that the pain would ease. Rather than weakening, the cramps intensified. Finally, sweating, I ran to the bathroom with an attack of diarrhea, then another and another until the pain was gone. Shaking and weak, I picked up the telephone on the wall and dialed home. It rang five times.

"Hello." I sagged with relief at Mom's voice.

"I'm sick and I need to come home," I whispered.

"What's the matter? You've only been gone a couple of hours."

"Can someone please come and get me," I begged.

"Are you okay?" Her voice rose.

"I'm sick and I need to come home."

After I hung up the telephone, Mr. Carter came out of his bedroom in his old-man undershirt and rumpled shorts. "I heard you on the phone." His voice was subdued. His earlier tone of bravado, mixed with sexual innuendo, was gone.

"I'm not well. I have to go home."

I changed back into my slacks and blouse in the bathroom, neatly folded up the blankets on the chesterfield, and sat down to wait. My tension unwound now that safety was on the way. Mr. Carter slumped on the chesterfield across from me.

"I've been so worried about my wife's operation." His words swirled meaninglessly around me. He hadn't said anything about her before. I kept my eyes on the door, contempt and loathing seething inside me.

Tom, a friend of my sister Sarah's, drove her over to pick me up. Sarah, home for a visit from Calgary, sat beside him in the front seat. Her blonde hair glowed in the darkness as she turned to face me in the back. "Thank you, thank you, for coming to get me," I babbled. "I was so scared. All he talked about was sex. He only mentioned his sick wife after I called home." Sarah reached over, patted my arm, and rested her hand on mine. Tom shook his head.

I went up the stairs to Mom and Dad's bedroom. I didn't care if they were mad at me for asking to come home because I was sick. Their light was off but their door was open. Shivering, I repeated what Mr. Carter had said to me. Mom shifted. Dad lay quiet. When I finished, I was light-headed.

"It's late, you'd better go to bed," Mom said. Dad didn't say anything.

I crawled into the safety of my bed and tucked the covers around me. I lay awake in the dark mugginess, trembling and cold, then feverish. My mind went over every detail of the evening, from the moment Dad told Brother Roy he could take me to babysit for his neighbor. I wanted to cry but no tears came. When daylight showed outside the bedroom curtains, my body still vibrated.

The next day, neither Mom nor Dad said anything to me about Mr. Carter. Not that night or anytime after. It was as if the evening had never happened.

The Pool Hall

A NEON SIGN in yellow and white, Seymour Billiards, flashed against the night sky, rotating above the entrance to the building. I paused, trembling. Was a billiard hall a den of iniquity? Should I call home to find out if it was okay to go in?

"It'll be fine," Don said. "I'm sure it'll be fine. It's just a pool hall. And we'll only play one game. It's still early. I don't want the evening to end. I haven't seen you all summer."

I hadn't told him what time I was supposed to be home. I was too embarrassed. It was such a ridiculously early curfew for a sixteen-year-old. Dad had given me permission to go the movie *Butch Cassidy and the Sundance Kid* with Don, playing in downtown Vancouver. "Make sure you're home by ten o'clock," Dad said as I went out the kitchen door. Mom followed up with, "The devil starts work at midnight."

We sat in the back row in the muggy darkness of the theater, holding hands and snuggling as close as we could, with the arm-rest separating us. Don was all I'd thought about for the past two months. He had just flown back from Moresby Island, not even taking the time to unpack at his grandmother's or do his laundry before riding over on his motorcycle to surprise me.

When I heard his Yamaha rev down the driveway, I dashed out the kitchen door, a dish towel still in my hand. "Is it you? Is it really you?" I wanted to jump up and down. I laughed as I hugged him. "I didn't expect you back until next week."

"I couldn't last any longer. I just about quit and came home when I got your letter about your Dad sending you to babysit at that creep's house. Anything could have happened to you. Anything. I

169

was sick to my stomach when I read what you went through." He held onto me and squeezed tight. "I'm just thankful you're okay." His voice choked and his blue eyes moistened.

When we came out of the Vogue Theatre on Granville Street, heat bounced off the pavement in waves. With summer soon over, the days were getting shorter. At nine o'clock it was already dark. Lights from the sidewalk cafes and bistros spilled onto the street. Carefree laughter and the chatter of people all dressed up on their way to nightclubs surrounded us.

Now I stood outside Seymour Billiards with Don, hesitating. I wasn't sure if it was okay to go in to begin with, and if he didn't take me straight home, I wouldn't make Dad's curfew. A couple of scenarios ran through my mind. One, Dad flying into a rage and yelling at me. I could handle that. I was sure I was too old for him to take his belt to me. Two, Dad forbidding me to ever go out with Don again. I couldn't imagine him doing that, but when he was angry there was no predicting. Still, if he did, he would cool down and forget about it in a couple of days. It would be as if nothing had ever happened.

On the plus side, even though Don wasn't a Mormon, Dad liked him. "Give him time," I overheard Dad say to Mom after my first date with Don. "If he's serious about Maggie, he'll be willing to take missionary lessons." Don had helped Dad fix fences one Saturday in the spring after we started dating. And he was going to BCIT. Dad respected that.

My desire to spend more time with Don won over my fear of Dad. We went inside. It took a minute for my eyes to adjust to the cigarette haze in the cavernous room. The crack of pool balls banged in my ears and the stench of spilled beer and stale sweat hung in the air. A snack bar was lit up at the back of the room. I saw a few women among the small groups of men clustered around the tables. They wore short cotton skirts that showed off their legs and tight, spaghetti-strap tops that hugged the curves of their breasts. Most of the men had on plaid cowboy shirts with the sleeves rolled up. Half-smoked cigarettes dangled from their lips.

Mom's voice in my head said low class.

I'd never played pool before. I'd never even seen a pool table except in movies, although I knew that Glynnis Davies in my class at school had one in her basement. The popular kids went over to her house after school to play.

"I'll give you a demonstration first," Don said. He carefully selected two sticks, called cues, from a rack on the wall and measured one against the height of my shoulder. "Okay, first you rack the balls, then you break with the white. The goal is to hit all the colored balls into the pockets with the white one. Hold the cue like so." Don placed his arms around me and his hands over mine. He drew the cue back and smacked the white ball right in the center. With his arms encircling me, I felt safe and loved.

Riding home on his motorcycle, I leaned against him and hugged his waist. We fit together like puzzle pieces. The last place I wanted to go was home. The warm wind on my face didn't quiet the fear building inside me.

I had always obeyed Mom and Dad, even though I hated my life since our move to Richmond. I kept my feelings about the church to myself in public, although if Mom actually listened to me at home, she had to be aware of what I thought. At church I went through the motions, aware that my behavior reflected on Mom and Dad. With Dad in the bishopric, maintaining the image of a devout family was critical.

I went to church meetings twice on Sunday, Seminary each morning before school, Mutual for teenagers one night a week, and every church event that Mom and Dad wanted me to. I played the piano on Saturday morning for the little kids to sing at Primary, and I paid tithing on my babysitting money. I dutifully did all my chores at home and stayed off school to take care of Mom whenever she was sick or needed help. It wasn't as if I had a choice about any of it: my fear of Dad kept me compliant. Tonight, I had claimed something for myself, something for me rather than for Mom and Dad. In our family, we children were there to meet Mom and Dad's needs; they were not there as parents to meet ours. Except for Janice.

Don pulled into the driveway just before eleven o'clock. The back porch light was out and the only light on the driveway was the white circle of the bike's headlight. He turned off the engine and balanced the bike as I climbed off. Crickets chirped in the warm darkness. "I hope your Dad's not going to mind that I took you to the pool hall." I leaned against him, my head on his shoulder, and wished we had more time. "I don't want to be the one to get you into any trouble." His breath against my ear joined me to him. "Do you want me to come in and talk to him?"

"No, no, it's not a big deal. I'll be just fine." My churning stomach told me otherwise. I handed him my helmet and kissed him a slow goodnight. His Old Spice aftershave wrapped around me. He kicked the bike into life and I watched the red taillight get smaller and smaller. Then I went in to face Dad.

Mom and Dad were still up. Dad lounged at the table in the kitchen, his sock feet up on a chair, the *Sun* newspaper spread out in front of him. Mom sat across from him with one of her church magazines open on her lap. I blinked at the brightness of the overhead light. The ticking of the clock on the wall thundered in my ears. Dad cleared his throat and looked up from the newspaper. The page in his hand cracked, loud, sharp. "What took you so long?" His eyes moved to the clock.

In a flash, an invisible knowing prompted me. My whole body trembled, but I couldn't let on, couldn't show any fear to feed the bully in Dad. My eyes met his. "Oh," I said nonchalantly over the hammering of my heart. "The time just got away on us. The movie was great, I think you'd enjoy it, and then we stopped off at Seymour Billiards. Don wanted to show me how to play pool, but I didn't really like the game. It was kind of a low-class place." Dad's eyes held mine for a moment, expressionless, then dropped back to the paper.

I walked past him and Mom, down the hall beside the living room and up the stairs to my bedroom. Behind my closed door I shook even more. Relief mixed with surprise zinged through me.

I hadn't thought, hadn't planned, just followed my gut. Did Dad comprehend what had just happened? I was just figuring it out myself. By pretending not to care about his response, there hadn't been any. I hadn't cowered, hadn't shown any fear. On a primal level, I had challenged the power Dad took for granted with my own. He was a bully who preyed on those weaker. I would still have to pick my battles carefully. On my first round, I had held my own.

Pimped Out

DONNA PUSHED HER WAY through the crowded hallway of Richmond High to my locker after the last bell rang. "I'm glad I caught you before you left. You're going to the track tonight, right?" She pushed her blonde hair behind one ear and leaned against the locker beside mine. The hem of her skirt ended mid-thigh. Mine reached to the dimple in the middle of my knee. Mom wouldn't let me wear miniskirts. It set me apart from most of the girls at school.

Donna's eyes never left the boys streaming past. She had just broken up with Mike, her boyfriend from the Vancouver ward. Some of the boys smiled and nodded at her. Donna grinned back. A few whistled. She ignored those, even though she enjoyed it. After they passed, a smile crept over her face.

When it came to attention from boys at school, I might as well have been invisible, except to Alex, who belonged to the chess club and whom I considered a geek. I didn't mind that the boys weren't interested in me. They all acted too young and I already had a boyfriend. All I thought about was Don. He had moved back to live with his parents in Gibsons and work at the pulp mill in Port Mellon. When he came into town, he stayed in his old room at his grandparents. We went to movies, to the A&W for hamburgers, or to the Dairy Queen for ice cream. Sometimes all we did was ride around on his motorcycle.

"Mom's going to drive me tonight. Do you need a ride?" I hollered to Donna over the din of voices and laughter.

"Do you think she'd mind?"

"Of course not. I'm sure we can swing by and pick you up. I'll

175

phone you." Even though it was Thursday and I had Seminary before school the next day, I was working an evening shift from six to ten o'clock in the concession at Paterson Race Track in Ladner. I had worked there twice a week for the past two months. There were races on Tuesday, Thursday, and Saturday nights. The ward had a contract to staff the booth with servers. The church was paid, not me. It was no use protesting. It was another one of those things that just was. It didn't matter how I felt about it or what I wanted. Mom and Dad had volunteered me to the money-making scheme for the church building fund.

"Maggie can go," Dad said with a satisfied smile, the same words he had said to Brother Roy about babysitting for his neighbor. Again, he had committed me without asking me first. The summer before, I had worked at a concession at the Pacific National Exhibition in Vancouver. The church had a contract with one of the vendors to staff his booth with teenage girls. Here we were again with the same arrangement, this time with the race track.

I said goodbye to Donna and hopped on the transit bus that dropped me at my stop for the mile walk home. Moat-like ditches and farmers' fields lined one side of River Road and the dyke lined the other. A narrow access road led onto the embankment. There were no cars in sight, either on the dyke or on the road. I relaxed.

The fall before, eleven-year-old Michael was attacked on the dyke at dusk, riding his bike home from a baseball practice. A man grabbed him, pulled him off his bike, and tried to tear his jeans off. Michael fought him off and ran home, barely able to speak. I was babysitting and called Mom and Dad at their church meeting. "I think you should come home."

After Michael's attack, every time I walked from the bus stop my body tensed and my eyes darted in all directions. I was primed to run. Sometimes there was a car with the windows steamed up parked on the dyke. I assumed it was a couple necking and ignored it. Every so often, there was a parked car with a single man behind the steering wheel. I was sure he was watching and waiting.

Adrenaline screamed through me and I ran the rest of the way home without stopping. If a car on the road drove too slowly, I scrambled up to the dyke and tore home.

I walked down the deserted road, with no danger in sight, taking my time and enjoying the warm sun. A slight breeze off the water carried the scent of river mud and salt from the nearby ocean. I didn't want to work the evening shift at the track, but even though I was tired, I would have to go. Maybe the excitement there would revive me. It was always busy and the time sped by. It could be fun gossiping with the other girls and giggling over all the older men who ogled and tried to pick us up.

At home, I hung out the laundry Mom had washed earlier, made a raspberry jam sandwich for supper, changed into a fresh blouse, and went out to the car. Dad was still at work. We swung by Donna's house on our drive down to Ladner. Traffic through the Deas Island Tunnel was slow and we got to the race track just before six o'clock. "I'll be back to pick you up at ten. Come straight out." Both Donna and I wore black skirts, white blouses, and sneakers, and we carried purses.

I paused on the curb and watched the station wagon disappear. Vehicles poured off the highway into the parking lot. Car doors slammed. The air throbbed with electricity and a chaotic hum began to build. In an hour it would reach a peak and hold.

"How come Janice never works at the track?" Donna asked as we walked to the admission gates. The hot scent of anxious horses and dust from the track flowed with us. My pulse quickened at the horses' high-pitched, excited whinnies.

"Her homework comes first." I was suddenly angry at Janice and at Mom and Dad.

"What about *your* homework?" Donna asked. I didn't answer. I couldn't put my hurt into words. I had lived with the unfairness for as long as I could remember. It was another one of those things that just was.

Paterson Race Track had a half-mile circuit for harness racing. The hooves of standardbred racers and trotters pounded around

177

the course. There were eight races a night. The drivers wore goggles and rode low behind the horses in two-wheeled carts. Depending on the weather, the drivers got covered in dust or spattered with mud.

The track swarmed with promoters, horse breeders, owners, trainers, grooms, drivers, handlers, veterinarians, punters, and racing aficionados. The aficionados all wore the same style of plaid sports jacket, with fedoras or flat tweed caps. They all had to eat. Most of them stopped at the concession to grab a greasy burger and fries or a hot dog and then rush back to the barns or stands with a "See ya later, babe."

As we wove through the groups of people holding betting sheets, Donna rolled the waistband of her skirt over a turn, hiking her miniskirt up even higher. I raised my eyebrows. "So?" Her blue eyes sparked. "Who do you think you are anyway? Somebody's mother?" She pushed my shoulder and we burst out laughing.

Even though she was a Mormon, Donna loved fashion. Her mother, a convert to the church, didn't think there was anything wrong with miniskirts. Mom wanted me to dress as if I were wearing temple garments in preparation for the day she planned that I would. My clothes were cumbersome and restrictive. I wasn't allowed to wear sleeveless dresses or blouses. It was useless to protest. Donna's mother hadn't been to the temple. She didn't have a husband to take her. Only older women who went on missions for the church were allowed to go to the temple without a husband. Donna's mom wore sleeveless blouses and short shorts.

The concession booth was below the stands. It was a long, narrow room with an open half-wall facing the track, topped with a serving counter covered in red-checked oilcloth. My mouth watered at the smell of onions sizzling on the grill.

Melanie and Sophie, two of the younger girls from the ward, fourteen and fifteen, were already at the booth. Melanie, brown-haired and sturdy, lived on a farm close by and was used to hard work. Sophie had beautiful black hair, milky skin, and a fragile look. Her mother was mentally ill and in Crease Clinic in Coquitlam.

Even though Sophie was a year older than Melanie, she was unsure of herself and easily distracted. We all kept an eye on her and helped her out with her orders.

The two girls had their hair pulled away from their faces in ponytails, rather than wearing hairnets to satisfy the health regulations. They had already tied on white aprons and were setting out the boxes of sugar cubes and cans of evaporated milk for the coffee. I pulled an elastic hair tie out of my purse and stowed my bag in the box with the rest of the purses under the counter. Donna's blonde hair already cascaded in a *I Dream of Jeannie* do from the top of her head.

Men milled around at the bottom of the stands and ogled us whenever they walked by. Some of the older men, with bags under their eyes and paunches rolling over their belts, stopped at the concession. Even if they were only buying a coffee, they would pull a wad of bills out of their pocket, lick their thumb, and peel a large bill off the roll.

Donna was an expert at resisting the steady stream of advances from the men.

"Just ignore them," she instructed Melanie and Sophie from behind the safety of the counter every time we worked together. "Some of them are real sleazebags. Don't give them any encouragement. Be polite when you serve them and nothing more. The trick is not to look them in the eye." None of the men, young or old, interested me. What did were the leftover hot dogs and hamburgers I ate free at end of the night when we cleaned up.

The announcer's voice boomed over the loudspeaker at the grandstand, "And here they come, warming up the track, getting ready for the night. *Lover Boy* with his driver Randy Nichols, *Prancing Lady* with Sam Raymond, *Sure to Place* . . ." His voice filled the stadium with the names of the horses and the odds on each. Forty-five minutes to gate time. Tensions rose. Everything began to spin.

My view of the race circuit was blocked by wall-to-wall people. I pasted a smile on my face, grabbed an order book, and turned to face a line of customers. Their voices and the rising noise in the

179

stadium blurred into one as I dashed to fill orders. When the first race started, there was a brief lull.

Halfway through the night, I glanced over at Donna. One of the promoters had stopped by to talk, his third time that evening. I noticed him because he stood off to the side and waited while she finished with a customer. He was dark-haired and handsome. His trousers were expensive and pressed with a knife-edge crease. His shirt underneath his sports jacket was crisp, not rumpled like the other men's. He had to be at least twenty-five or thirty. I checked for a wedding band. Of course, even though his ring finger might be bare, he could still be married.

"Are you busy after work?" I heard him ask Donna.

She giggled. "You mean after I do my homework?"

I peered at him out of the corner of my eye and tried to listen to him, to Donna, and to a customer's order all at the same time. "What a kidder you are," he said. "Seriously, I've been watching you. I want to take you out."

"No can do. My friend's mom is picking me up." She turned away.

"Hey, no, wait a minute." There was a pleading tone in his voice. "If you want to go out sometime, anytime, another time that suits you, *you* could call me. I'll take you somewhere nice. We can go to dinner or dancing or . . . You can invite a friend to come along if you want."

Donna half-turned. She hesitated, confusion flashing across her face. He pulled a napkin out of one of the containers and jotted something down, then slid the napkin across the counter to her. She turned to face him.

I gasped. She wasn't going to consider calling him, was she? She was the one who warned us about the men at the track. He was much too old for her—and he wasn't a Mormon. I bet he smoked and drank, maybe even used drugs. A fast crowd hung out at the track. Some had even been to jail. My mouth dropped open as I watched.

Donna picked up the napkin, gave him a tentative smile, and

tucked it into the waistband of her apron. I couldn't believe what she'd just done. At the end of our shift, she caught my eye and laughed. She pulled the napkin out of her apron, made a show of crumpling it up and holding it high above the garbage can, and dropped it in.

Four weeks later, on the front page of the weekly *Richmond Review* was the promoter who had tried to pick up Donna. There he was, in a feature-size crowd shot, lying on the flattened grass at a weekend music festival at Minoru sports field. Cradled in his arms was Sophie, and in her fingers was what looked like a marijuana joint.

Temptation

I ARRIVED IN BANFF on the overnight bus from Vancouver, groggy with exhaustion. Sleep had been impossible. Every time the bus stopped to pick up freight or passengers, the gears hissed and the seat underneath me shuddered. My initial excitement at escaping from home and mandatory church attendance was gone. I stumbled into the depot bleary-eyed. No one was meeting me.

Janice was at work on the morning shift at the Cascades Hotel coffee shop. She had come up in May, the month before, at the end of her first year at the University of British Columbia. At seventeen, I had just finished grade eleven. Mom, who had worked as a nanny for a wealthy Mormon family in Banff thirty years before, had encouraged me to join her. After trying every few years since I was twelve, she had finally found me a live-away situation for the summer. For two months, she wouldn't have to field my questions about the church.

At the bus depot in Banff, fear grabbed my stomach but there was no going home. I stowed my suitcase in one of the lockers on a side wall, visited the washroom, and dabbed at my face with a dampened paper towel. My heart knocked against my ribs as the attendant at the ticket desk gave me directions to the employment office.

Outside, I gasped in the chill mountain air that must have been below freezing. Rising sun reflected off the jagged, snow-topped mountain peaks rimming the town, and fluffy clouds floated against an emerging blue sky. I shivered, overwhelmed by the magnificence, but also with cold. My thin jacket, jeans, and sneakers weren't warm enough. At home in Richmond the days were hot, with strawberries already ripe in the fields.

A rustic log building a few streets from the bus depot housed the government employment agency. Crusty patches of old snow lay on the ground among stretches of stamped-down, brown grass. Two German shepherds tied to a rail in front strained at their leashes, howling and yapping. The building and dogs reminded me of a frontier town in a Wild West movie rather than a tourist resort in the Rocky Mountains in the late 1960s.

I paused, took a breath, and walked through the door. Waves of patchouli, musty wool, and unwashed bodies slammed into me. Young people, mainly college students, milled around the foyer. Backpacks rested against the walls here and there. I had to be the youngest person in the room. Everyone stared at me in my light summer clothing. Shaking with nerves and cold, I grabbed one of the applications from a stack inside the door, filled it out, and approached the clerk.

The woman, whose glasses dangled from a chain around her neck, smiled at me from behind the counter. She slipped her glasses onto her nose and reviewed the application I slid meekly across to her. I had listed my experience at the concession booths at the Paterson Race Track and Pacific National Exhibition. I didn't specify that it had been for the church; I simply wrote down the length of time at each and my duties.

"Check out the notices on the board," she instructed, as if reading from a script. "Come back in the morning at ten o'clock. You're too young to work in a dining room because they serve liquor. You have to be twenty-one for that, but there are coffee shops that need waitresses."

I blinked and swallowed, my face hot. What if no one hired me? I didn't have enough money for bus fare home. Her voice softened. "The hotels all check in here first thing in the morning. I'll be able to find you something by tomorrow and send you out to work. All the hotels are short-staffed right now." Relief surged through me.

She added, "Do you have a place to stay?"

I nodded. "My sister's here and she's found a room for both of us."

Janice didn't get off work till early afternoon. I wandered in and out of all the gift stores and galleries. As soon as Janice glimpsed me on the sidewalk outside the hotel, her face lit up. "Whew! Thank goodness. I wondered where you were. Why didn't you come in and say hi as soon as you got in?"

"I wasn't sure if it was okay."

She shook her head and made a face. "All you had to do was stick your head in the door and wave." My chest tightened over causing her to worry and with embarrassment at my shyness.

"Well, I didn't know." Despite the patronizing way she talked to me, there were moments when I was sure she loved me and would do what she could to champion me. Before Dad's beating when I was five, I had been the one who knocked on doors for both us while she hung back. Afterward, she was the one who took the lead.

Janice lived at a rooming house. For us, she had rented a basement room with two beds at the Hansens, a young Mormon family who lived on Wolfe Street close to downtown. We could move in the following afternoon. Just before we reached her rooming house, she grabbed my suitcase. "I don't want the landlady to catch you carrying a suitcase. We're not allowed overnight guests. If she sees me with it, I'll make up something about my move."

The building, a thirties' style, was at the end of town by a bridge. Above the entrance of the two-story structure, a sign in bold lettering read: "Absolutely No Overnight Guests." I gulped.

Janice had a single bed with an old-fashioned metal frame in a room on the ground floor she shared with three French Canadian girls. "You're going to have to sleep with me." She put my suitcase beside her bed. "Good thing it's only for one night. Banff doesn't have enough summer accommodations."

Every time I crept out of the room to use the bathroom in the hall, I was sure the landlady would come down from her suite upstairs. "What if she catches me?" I asked Janice.

"Don't worry about her now you're inside. Keep your voice down and everything will be fine. If we hear her on the stairs, hide under the bed." When Janice turned off the light, I squeezed flat on my back underneath her bed, breathing in dust and trying not to sneeze. I could barely move. The wire bedsprings were inches from my face. "What are you doing that for now?" Janice hissed. "She's not going to come down at night." Her roommates giggled. I wasn't taking any chances.

Halfway through the night, cold and unable to sleep, I crawled out from under the bed and squished in beside Janice. It wasn't any better. I lay rigid and awake, worried about falling onto the floor, getting a job, and how churchy the Hansens would be.

In the morning at eight o'clock, tired and without any breakfast, I shivered on the steps outside the employment office. The doors opened at eight-thirty and a clerk told me to wait on one of the chairs. Heat blasting from the radiators thawed my hands and feet. Half an hour later, a middle-aged woman named Irene introduced herself as the coffee shop manager for the Rimrock Hotel. After a couple of questions she hired me. I sagged with relief and laughed at my anxiety.

"Can you start tomorrow? You can drive up with me now to pick up your uniforms. Morning shift starts at seven o'clock and the afternoon shift at three-thirty. Have you got any preference?"

"Either shift is fine, but I'd prefer to work every Sunday." I was short of breath as I said the words. She stared at me for a moment. I swallowed.

"I'll remember that when I make up the schedule," she finally said. Free at last to make the choice of not going to church, my whole being danced. For the first time in my life, I said what I wanted and no one told me I was wrong. A sense of sureness expanded within me and a stillness settled in. I could eat all my meals at work, and with working on Sundays I would hardly see or have to explain anything to the Hansens. They had never met Mom and Dad and wouldn't be able to tell on me. Janice could be trusted not to say anything. Now that she was going to university and lived away from home, she was no longer caught up in a competition to get what she wanted from Mom and Dad. I doubted that whether I went to church was of any significance to her. Just like Rob and Sarah, she had moved on in her life. There was nothing for her at home. Mom and Dad and the house we lived in embarrassed her.

That afternoon when Janice finished work, we lugged our suitcases over to the Hansens' house. Janice had met them at church. They were a friendly young couple who had just gotten out of university and had a toddler and a new baby. Brother Hansen managed a gift store and Sister Hansen was a stay-at-home mom.

Our rented room in the basement was a short flight of steps from the split-level entrance at the front of the house. The walls were paneled in rec-room walnut and floral curtains covered the windows. A full bathroom was across the hall.

After Sister Hansen showed us to the room, she stood in the hallway outside our door, poised to go upstairs. "The front door's always unlocked, so come and go as you want. If you come in late, please close the door quietly. We go to bed early." Happiness surged inside me. She hadn't asked any questions about the church or even mentioned it. Living with the Hansens was going to suit me just fine.

The following morning, my first day of work, I was on the seven o'clock shift. The Rimrock Hotel, located above the town, sent a station wagon down to the Rundle Cafe on Banff Avenue to pick up staff. The Rundle was a two-minute walk from the Hansens. I waited for the car beside the steps of the cafe in the crisp dawn air, wearing my new gold-colored uniform, a sweater, and my jacket. Towering mountains surrounded me. I was small and insignificant in comparison. Two young women who worked as chars cleaning rooms at the hotel waited with me.

On the ten-minute drive up the winding mountain road, deer and moose loped in front of the car and into the woods. Douglas fir, white spruce, and pine trees formed a wall on either side of the road. The scenery blurred by as I went over Irene's instructions from the day before.

The Rimrock hung on the edge of a cliff overlooking the Banff Springs Hotel, a golf course, and a tree-lined crevasse. Across the road on the upper side was the Banff Upper Hot Springs. Some of the older hotel guests stayed for the whole summer to visit the hot springs and ease the pain of their arthritis in the hot mineral waters.

I pushed open the glass door of the coffee shop to the acrid aroma of percolating coffee. The steaming liquid gurgled and dripped from the machine into a beaker on the hot plate below. Linda, one of the waitresses I'd met at the hotel the day before, raised her head and smiled as she wiped up spilled coffee grounds on the counter. "All ready for your first day?" She was slight and pretty and her blonde hair was pulled back in a ponytail. The best I could do was smile and nod.

"Put your purse and jacket in the back and I'll show you how to fill the juices. You'll soon get the hang of it." Linda glanced around, as if checking to make sure we were alone. "The gorbies are easy to please, just as long as their coffee's strong and ready."

"Gorbies?"

She laughed. "Tourists. Gorbies are what we call them behind their backs."

Linda and Jeannie, the other waitress, kept an eye out for me and gave me cues throughout the morning. They coached me as they rushed to and from the kitchen. I worked behind the counter filling coffee and soft drink orders and making milkshakes. In the afternoon I started waiting on tables. By the end of my shift, I had slipped into a comfortable routine.

On my second afternoon, I dashed into the prep area behind the coffee shop and nearly fell over a man crouched beside one of the bottom cupboards, blocking my way to the kitchen. "Oops. Sorry." I flushed with embarrassment.

"No, no, I was in *your* way." The man stood up slowly, smiled, and laughed out loud. All the breath went out of me. He had wavy black hair and brown eyes and spoke with a European accent. "I'm Charles, bartender in the lounge. I search for small napkins.

You must be new." For a moment I couldn't speak; I just stared at his lopsided grin.

Before he started work each day, he came into the coffee shop and chatted with all the waitresses. Every time, my heart sped up. He was either thirty or thirty-two; his answer was different the two times I asked. "I'm an artist. I come from Hungary eight years ago. I bartend to earn money." I had never met anyone so exotic. I wanted to find out everything about him.

Brewster Bus tours frequently stopped at the hot springs across the street, and when they did, every seat in the coffee shop filled with tourists expecting instant service. That was the time I was sure to screw up—to forget to add chips to an order or fail to write down that a hamburger was to be plain with no cheese. I raced back and forth between customers, unable to please everyone at the same time.

Lee, the cook, short and close to retirement age, usually joked around—except when a tour was in. "For Chrissakes, why can't you get it right the first time, girl?" he snarled at me. "You want a new burger? Just scrape the cheese off yourself, goddammit." He scowled and shook his head so hard that the white envelope of a cap he wore slipped sideways on his bald head. That made him even madder.

I watched Linda and Jeannie and the other waitresses and copied how they dealt with Lee when they screwed up. I learned from them that Lee was all bluff. The first few times I stuck up for myself, I was nervous. After that, even though my stomach clenched, I talked to him the same way they all did. It got easier. When he yelled at me, I hollered back, scowling as he did, "I need a fresh burger with no cheese. Give me a break. It's not about me, it's the customer." Other times, in the right, I defended myself. "Can I help it if the customer changed their mind and wants a Denver now instead of a clubhouse? Got nothin' to do with me." I was smug then and sure of myself. At the same time, I marveled at the words that came out of my mouth. Was that really me speaking?

Some days, when the tour buses stopped and a mob of people

rushed through the door, battling each other for a table, I stifled the impulse to run and hide until they all left. I fantasized about untying my apron and slipping out the back door. Then I reminded myself how quickly the pockets in my uniform would sag with their tips.

Back in my room at the Hansens, I emptied my tips onto my narrow bed beside Janice's. Counting the silver coins and bills, usually more than my wages, was satisfying: I had never had so much money. There was no one wanting a share, and Mom wasn't here to force me to pay tithing. As soon as I had earned enough to pay the Hansens for rent, and for odds and ends, I opened a bank account at the Bank of Montreal to save for university.

If Janice wasn't in the room, I took out the letters from Don hidden in my suitcase in the closet. In my first weeks at Banff, I'd written him every day. The letters he'd sent me were creased and smudged from reading them again and again. That was before my feelings for Charles developed. Whenever Charles came into the coffee shop, electricity zapped through me. I still wrote to Don, although my stomach twisted with the guilt of my secret, and my letters were short.

One afternoon at the end of July before he opened the lounge, Charles asked, "Have you got a minute?" His teeth flashed his signature smile. "I want to show you something." I followed him up the service stairs, trembling, sure I was doing wrong by going to a forbidden zone. I was too young to go into the lounge when it was open, and according to the church, it was an evil place whether open or closed. Everything in the room glittered. Chrome-backed stools with white leather seats lined a long shiny bar. Behind, on a mirrored wall, were rows of liquor bottles. The sun through the floor-to-ceiling windows bounced off the mirror in blinding flashes. Beyond the windows, jagged mountains soared into a blue sky from the tree-lined valley below. Charles proudly lifted the cover off an easel set up in front of the windows. The mountain scene on the canvas replicated the view perfectly.

As I admired his painting he moved close. His pine aftershave enveloped me in waves of pleasure. I swayed, overwhelmed, and ran back down the stairs to the coffee shop. Charles chuckled behind me. The scent of his aftershave stayed with me for the rest of my shift. In bed that night, I wrapped the moments in the lounge around me until I finally slept.

Whenever Charles came into the coffee shop after that, he complimented me on my curves. "Ah, it's good you're putting on weight. When you started you were so skinny," or "You begin to look womanly. We European men admire women who are robust, like good wine." He brought his fingers to his lips, kissed them, then opened his hand.

In June, I had worn a size-twelve uniform. Now, after a month of eating bacon and eggs at work every morning, carrot cake with cream cheese icing on my breaks, veal cutlets with mashed potatoes and gravy, or towering clubhouse or grilled ham-and-cheese sandwiches, with soup *and* salad for lunch and supper, I had changed up to a size fourteen. I felt pudgy but hadn't been able to resist the food. I could eat as much as I wanted for free. The variety and abundance was a striking contrast to the food from the garbage dump at home.

Each day I surveyed my uniformed body in the mirror and wondered what Charles thought when he watched me. I imagined us kissing, our bodies pressed together, drowning in the scent of him. When he was due to arrive at work, my every nerve was raw, on alert, waiting. If he didn't stop in, I slumped in despair, sure he wasn't interested in me anymore.

His seduction began in earnest one afternoon in August, in the lull between the lunch and dinner rush. I was sitting on a bar stool in the prep area, the rung digging into my stocking feet. A pile of laundered serviettes lay in front of me. Jeannie, who was on evening shift with me, was out front with the customers.

Hands touched my shoulders. I jumped. The faint scent of cigars and brandy mixed with pine aftershave whooshed around me. It was Charles's fingers that lifted my hair and caressed my neck. I bit back a moan. Warm breath blew on the back of my neck and

191

soft lips brushed my skin. I tilted my head forward hoping for more.

"Hi there, babe." His deep male voice was close to my ear.

I went all weak. I didn't want him to stop. I knew I should be angry at him for touching and kissing me, but I wasn't. I liked it too much.

"Why don't you visit my apartment across the street after work?" he whispered. "Don't take shuttle down at end of your shift. I meet you in lobby. I'll drive you home."

I turned to face him. His black hair receded on his forehead and there were fine lines spreading from the edges of his brown eyes. His skin was tanned. He wore a soft burgundy jacket buttoned on the right and dress pants with a crease that broke over glistening, black leather shoes. His lopsided grin, his foreignness, and his engaging laugh were intoxicating. My heart careened in my chest. I mutely shook my head. Misery at saying no flooded me.

I wanted so much to say yes, but I had watched how he flirted with the waitresses who worked in the dining room. They were over twenty-one, old enough to serve liquor and go up to the lounge whenever they wanted, which I was sure they did after the dining room closed. A few of the single women guests at the hotel were giddy after their evenings in the lounge. They ate breakfast in the coffee shop and talked and giggled with flushed faces about Charles. Some had no doubt gone over to his apartment; or maybe he had even gone to their rooms. I smiled politely as I served them, burning with jealousy and calling them unspeakable names in my mind.

Despite all the women who glowed when he was around, I still waited for Charles's hands on my shoulders when he crept up behind me in the prep area. I wanted to believe he loved me when he whispered, "I'm going crazy thinking about you, babe. Please say yes before I lose more sleep."

Charles was all I thought about—at work, off work, and when I closed my eyes at night. As August drew to a close, he became more serious. When he caught up with me in the coffee shop, he tried to persuade me to go away with him.

"Have you thought about coming to Waterton Lakes with me at the end of the season? It's only a few hours' drive," he reminded me in his gravelly voice. Every time I heard him I could barely breathe.

"I get you a job waitressing, easy," he cajoled. "Why you want to go back to school? You want to see the world, don't you? I'm the guy to show it to you."

"Am I the only one you've asked?" My gut told me I wasn't.

"Babe, you're the only one I even think of asking. What do I have to do to make you believe me? You're all I want. You're special."

Against all reason, I wanted to believe him, oh, how I wanted. I considered the possibilities. I longed to go with Charles, even though it would be the same as jumping off a cliff blindfolded. He excited me, but he terrified me too. He had never said he loved me as Don had or talked about marriage. He had only talked about how much fun we could have together.

I was sure the intensity of my feelings for Charles was love. Even though I loved him, what kind of life could I have with him? He loved women, all types and ages. I couldn't be sure I would be the only one. Yet I didn't want to go back home. An ongoing struggle over the church awaited me there. The one person who was important to me, Don, had dwindled to a distant figure in my mind, only a frayed thread of a few random letters connecting us. While it was comforting to know he was still there, my feelings for him had changed. Maybe his for me had changed over the summer too.

Always there were the images and voices of my favorite teachers talking to me about going to university. "You're smart," every one of them had told me. "Don't waste it." I didn't have any desire to be a teacher or a nurse. Home economics teaching, which Janice was preparing for at UBC, and nursing were the only two professions, other than being a secretary, that Mom and Dad thought were acceptable. Although Sarah worked as a secretary, she was going to university at night to become a teacher. She was too busy to write to me anymore.

At the end of August, after we both finished a dayshift and changed into shorts, Janice and I ambled along Wolfe Street in the hot afternoon sun toward the A&W downtown. They had a self-serve soft drink machine and we made swamp water: root beer mixed with orange crush.

As we walked, I noticed that Janice's hair had grown longer over the summer. She held it back from her face with an elastic. We usually worked different shifts and hadn't spent much time together in the past two months. I'd never talked to her about Charles or, for that matter, about anything else that was important to me, although she knew I hated going to church. Anytime I'd tried to talk to her before, she'd frowned and asked, "Why are you telling me this?"

Now I asked her, "Do you ever want a different kind of life than you have? Do you ever think about not going back home to school? I mean, just staying on and when the season is over, going to work somewhere else or doing something entirely different?"

"Don't be silly," Janice snapped, exasperated. "Why would I want to do that? Why are you asking me something so stupid? Sometimes I worry about you." She shook her head.

Embarrassed, I bit my lip and didn't answer. I'd wanted to find out if she had ever been uncertain about anything, and what she had done about it. Instead, she talked to me as if *I* was stupid, not just my questions.

I was achingly alone. Before Banff, my life had centered rigidly on the church, helping out at home, and then school. That had all changed. There was no one I could talk to about the tug of war raging inside me. Should I go with Charles to Waterton Lakes? Or should I go back home and finish my last year of high school?

Homecoming

I SAID GOODBYE to Charles on my last afternoon at the Rim-rock Hotel. His lopsided grin was gone. We stood on the faded carpet in the prep area of the coffee shop. "Is there anything I can say to change your mind?" He gazed into my eyes and grasped my hands.

Every part of me trembled. I steadied myself against the counter as he hugged me and his lips brushed the side of my neck. I inhaled his pine aftershave and reminded myself that he was twice my age and was not a one-woman man. He finally turned and trudged up the service stairs. The pain in my chest made it hard to breathe. I wanted to run after him and call out, "Stop! Stop! I'll go with you. Please. Wait."

He didn't come to the train station the next morning. There was no reason to expect that he might, but I had still hoped. On the train trip from Banff through the mountains back to Vancouver, I hid behind sunglasses, leaned my cheek against the window, and replayed the sensation of his lips on my neck. My heart hurt. He would quickly find a new romance, if he hadn't already. Maybe one of the dining room waitresses who I was sure went across the street to his apartment. Or someone in Waterton.

Mom's words echoed with each chug and hiss of the engine, each blast of the whistle: "Raise up a child in the way he should go and he will not depart from it . . ." I was no better than a hom-ing pigeon: returning instinctively to what was familiar, unable to resist the pull of an inner magnet. Yet my decision to come home rather than run away to Waterton Lakes had nothing to do with scripture. Turning my back on school and on graduating had been too wrenching to contemplate. I wanted to graduate. And then there was Don. I didn't love him in the same way as before, but I still wanted to see him. Other than school, he was the only positive thing waiting for me.

For two blissful months, I had lived without fear, outside the reach of Mom, Dad, and the church. There had been no kneeling beside my chair before breakfast, no listening to prayers that dragged on until my knees ached, no early morning Seminary. In Banff, I hadn't attended a single Sunday service. It was freeing and downright amazing not to go to church. Each Sunday, a tiny twinge of guilt pinched me—but not for long.

When the train pulled into Vancouver, Don was waiting. He slouched against a railing, hands in his pockets, shirtsleeves rolled up to his elbows, a grin on his face. With his welcoming arms around me, I was immediately comforted. He smelled of the outdoors and sun. I relaxed into him, a loose puzzle piece fit back into place.

At home everything was the same but nothing felt right. It was as if I was wearing a sweater that was too small and choked my neck. Every Sunday morning after Dad left for priesthood meeting and before we went to Sunday school, my questions to Mom were the same as always, but now they were more thought-out and solid. With my graduation from high school and freedom from home and church in sight, Mom wasn't as dangerous as she once was. Two months of making my own choices, with no one telling me I was wrong, had changed me.

I washed the breakfast dishes while Mom swept the kitchen floor and got out her church books. "Why is it necessary to go to every church meeting?" I asked. "I'll soon be eighteen. How old does a person have to be to make their own choices?"

Mom's expression of exasperation—the rolling of the eyes, the pulling down of the mouth—was the same as before, yet it didn't affect me as it once had. Wielding the power conferred on her by Dad, handed down through the generations from Joseph Smith, she replied, "Because it's what your Heavenly Father and your father and mother here want you to do." Her voice, sharp and laced with the strength of the Mormon church, no longer pierced my soul. It was only a matter of time. While I was under Mom and Dad's roof, I had no choice but to follow their rules. It had come down to a choice between the freedom to make my own decisions—and family. Mom and Dad and the church were one.

Neither Mom nor Dad complained when I got a waitressing job at the Steak Pit in Richmond Centre, close to school. I worked the dinner shift on Thursdays and Fridays, and all day Saturday, and saved my wages and tips for university.

Careful to keep up my A and B grades at school, I skipped classes. If the sun was out or if Don was over from Gibsons for a visit, I took the afternoon off. Sometimes I snuck out when the bell rang for lunch and didn't go back. Other times, just to be on the safe side, I stopped in at the office and feigned illness. I was never doubted.

"Oh, I'm so sorry," Mrs. Neilson, the school secretary, said each time she listened to another malady, genuine concern on her face. I didn't fit the stereotype of a slacker or the liar I had become. I was one of the nice girls: modestly dressed, quiet, respectful. I didn't cause disruption in class and I turned in my homework on time. Invisible, really—the perfect student, though with delicate health, given all my absences despite my robust athletic appearance and pink cheeks.

"It's a pleasure to have Maggie in my class," my social studies teacher wrote on my first report card. I knew intuitively how to please. I had learned how to do it at home to keep myself safe from Dad. What to say, what not to say, and when to make myself scarce. It worked in my favor at school.

At church, there were plenty of opportunities to hone my chameleon skills. No one was interested in what I thought or who I was. Attending services was a dishonest act. The thought of being authentic, rather than the false, made-up person everyone wanted me to be, made me laugh bitterly, it was so unthinkable. The thirteenth article of faith, one of the statements setting out the basic tenets of the Mormon church, started off with "We believe in being honest, true . . ."

When I was baptized at eight, I had no idea what those words meant. I did now. When and where did the honesty happen? Everyone at church hid behind the same smile and acted the same way. I had never heard anyone challenge or question anything. Being honest and speaking up could get a member kicked out and split up a family. I had seen it happen with Bishop Simpson and his family, and Sister McGowan had left the church because of it.

Restlessness lived inside me. I wasn't sure about anything except that I wanted the freedom to think for myself and make my own choices. That wasn't possible living with Mom and Dad.

At Easter break, Uncle Denis, one of Dad's brothers, and his wife Aunt Helen visited. Uncle Denis was the dean of a college in the San Fernando Valley in California. Rob had lived with them after he served his mission while he studied to become a court reporter.

I had only seen Rob twice since he left home: once when he came home for a few days after being released from his mission and again when he married Ann, whom he'd met and converted to the church in Texas. There were no marriage festivities to look forward to, and none of us kids were allowed to go to their wedding at the temple. Our camping trip to Salt Lake City to stay with Aunt Letty and Uncle Barry, and to meet up with Rob and Ann, was all that marked the event. On the morning of their wedding in Salt Lake, Ann fasted in preparation for going to the temple for the first time and helped Mom and Aunt Letty can apricots. Ann and Rob, along with Mom and Dad and Aunt Letty and Uncle Barry, went to the temple in the afternoon for six or seven hours for the ceremony.

No one mentioned Ann's parents, who were non-Mormons. What did they think, especially her mother, about not being able to attend their only daughter's wedding? How did Ann feel about spending the morning of her wedding day canning apricots? Did she understand that it was a precursor to her life as a Mormon wife? After their marriage, Rob and Ann moved to Idaho, too far away to visit, just like Sarah, who had moved to Arizona and had yet to get married.

During Uncle Denis and Aunt Helen's visit, on Sunday evening after sacrament meeting, we squished into the station wagon and drove up to the top of Burnaby Mountain. Uncle Denis wanted to check out the new Simon Fraser University. It was concrete and glass, with sharp lines and open spaces, joined in a continuous square. Inside the frame was a flat green space bordering a shallow body of water.

"SFU is the leading edge in education as far as universities go today," Uncle Denis said. "It's all the talk at the conferences that I've been to lately." He was on a first-name basis with the chancellor. I hung onto his every word, as if he had spoken directly to me, and decided that night to apply for the fall semester. It was as if Uncle Denis had handed me the answer to my future.

The day my grad invitation from high school arrived in the mail, I showed it to Mom right away. She was in the kitchen as always. She went to the calendar tacked on the wall and flipped over the page to May, then turned to me. "Dad and I aren't going to be able to make it. He has a quarterly church meeting in Vancouver that night. It's not something he can miss."

"It doesn't matter," I said, thinking how uncomfortable I would be among my school friends and their parents and how embarrassed if Mom and Dad *did* come. I squirmed at the thought of Dad, without the weight of his church authority, grinning nervously, which he did when he wasn't comfortable. Maybe he'd even take out his pocket knife and clean his nails. That would be excruciating. I would be anxious, too, about Mom asking inappropriate questions about other people's choice of religion.

"It doesn't matter," I said again to Mom. "I'm probably not going to go myself anyway." I took the stairs two at a time to my room. It did matter. It mattered to me and I wanted it to matter to them. My graduation was the celebration of the completion of one part of my life and the beginning of the next. I wanted them to want to come, yet the church always came first. Our large family, the price of Mom and Dad's ticket to heaven, was a burden, an obligation, rather than a joy. We were inconsequential to them in comparison to the church. Only Rob and Janice appeared to matter to them, and both of them hardly kept in touch with Mom and Dad now.

Mom and Dad's lack of interest in my graduation ceremony rubbed raw scars from similar wounds. Hurt washed over me in one decimating wave after another. Maybe, I thought, maybe Mom and Dad plan to surprise me and make an exception about Dad's church meeting. Who was I kidding?

The morning of my graduation I lingered in bed, nestled in the warm cocoon of covers, and listened to the birds through my half-open window. The sun was bright and it was already warm. I imagined walking up the steps onto the stage in front of my schoolmates and their families to receive my diploma. I was sure I would be nervous with so many eyes on me. My stomach fluttered at the thought of my certificate being placed in my hand.

Mom was in the kitchen when I came downstairs. The smell of porridge cooking greeted me. I glanced at the counter and the table. There was no white envelope with my name on it, no small brown paper bag or wrapped gift. Mom and Dad had given Janice a watch when she graduated. Maybe they planned to give me something later.

"Will you make Michael and Ian lunches to take to school?" Mom asked as she stirred the porridge. "I baked bread yesterday. There should be peanut butter and jam, and I think there's still some apples in the crisper in the fridge. If there's only one left, just cut it in half." The brightness of the day dimmed.

In the evening, my friend Madeline and her parents picked me up for the ceremony. Dad had already left for his meeting. I wore my first store-bought dress, paid for with waitressing money. It was a stylish, light-blue cotton with a scalloped hemline and narrow matching belt. I had carefully applied makeup.

As I walked through the kitchen, Mom had a distracted expression on her face, as if noticing for the first time that there was something different about me. "You look pretty in that dress, dear. Have a nice evening." I swallowed the lump in my throat, smiled a church smile, and wished that my life was different.

In the muggy, semi-dark gymnasium beside Madeline and her parents, I wished that I hadn't come. Despite their kindness in picking me up, I was alone and out of place. They didn't comment on Mom and Dad's absence. I tried to distract myself from the emptiness inside by focusing on the chemical odor of the new wax on the floor and on the floral scent of corsages and boutonnieres. My schoolmates all glowed with a halo of happiness, the girls beautiful and the boys suddenly grown-up in their suits. Hushed coughs and whispers rippled through the auditorium.

A familiar loneliness expanded within me. Although Mom and Dad weren't coming, it had never occurred to me to invite anyone else. Both of my friends Madeline and Sandy were graduating too. Don, the other person who was important to me, was working at the pulp mill in Port Mellon. Rob and Sarah lived too far away. If they had been closer, I was sure they would have come. Inviting Janice hadn't even been a consideration. She hung out with her university friends and only talked to me when she wanted something. I was in a gymnasium full of people, but I was alone, unattached to anyone or anything. I floated without an anchor in an endless black space.

When the awards were announced, I ached with a raw, lingering regret. Not over Mom and Dad but for myself. If only I had worked harder, hadn't cut classes, had been more focused, I could have been one of the students up there receiving a scholarship.

When Madeline's parents dropped me off at home, Mom and Dad were already in bed and their light was out. There was no gift, no flowers, and no card waiting for me on the kitchen table or in my bedroom.

The third week of June, the letter from Simon Fraser University arrived in the mail. I stood in the morning sunshine beside the mailbox and savored the two sentences: "We acknowledge receipt of your application. The university welcomes you . . ." My hands trembled. Two honeybees buzzed around my ears and dive-bombed close to my face. I didn't bother flicking them away. It was only a form letter but that didn't take away from its promise. Excitement mixed with fear tingled through me. My acceptance into SFU would be finalized on receipt of my exam results. I wasn't worried about my grades. That wasn't the part that scared me.

With the letter in my hand, I rushed through the kitchen door. "Mom, Mom, I made it."

She stood at the counter with her back to me, gently tapping the bottom of a pan to tip out a warm loaf of bread. My eyes went to the knotted tie at her waist that held her apron in place. For a moment, I thought she hadn't heard me. She turned slowly. "That's nice, dear." There was no excitement in her voice.

My happiness plummeted. We sat at the table across from each other. "I was hoping . . . I was hoping," I swallowed. My face was on fire. "I was hoping that you and Dad would help me if I need it. I've got money saved from Banff and from waitressing at the Steak Pit. It should be enough for tuition and books for at least the first year. I can waitress and earn more." I drew in a breath. "For my first year, I want to take humanities courses."

Mom and Dad weren't poor anymore, even if we lived poor. Dad still worked at the landfill and received a regular paycheck from Burnaby municipality. He made money on the side from his salvage business. He also sold copper wire and metals left by the truck drivers, and he had kept up his cattle business.

Mom glanced down at her hands in her lap, at the floor, then over at the window. Why wasn't she answering? I had never asked for anything before. "We're helping Janice right now." Her words were measured and even. Yes, I was aware that they were paying for her room in a shared house near the UBC campus and buying her groceries; and I knew that they had bought her a black Volkswagen bug to drive. "I don't see how we can possibly help you too."

A pain started in the pit of my stomach. I blinked fast. It

spread to my chest. Mom hadn't said it, but they were still giving money to the church, just as they had always done. I grew smaller and smaller.

"There's something else I want to talk to you about." It was as if Mom's voice was coming through water. Blub, blub, blub . . . "Dad and I have just bought the acreage with the house and barn on it in Surrey that we looked at. We're putting the house here up for sale now that the renovations are finished." I knew they had looked at property but not that they had bought anything.

"We want you to stay home over the summer and help us get organized for the move. We'll need your help to settle into the new house." The sensation of floating in endless black space that I had had at my graduation ceremony overwhelmed me. "With Rob and Sarah gone and Janice working in Jasper for the summer," she went on in a neutral tone, "you're the only one we've got to help us."

Then her voice changed, became ingratiating, reached out as if to wrap itself around me and bind me to her. "You're such a good daughter. I don't know what I would have done without your help all these years. I've always been able to count on you . . ."

I suddenly felt the hard wood of the chair underneath my legs. The urge to scream without stopping surged through me. When I finally spoke, only the huskiness in my voice betrayed the frenzy seething inside. My hands twisted in my lap and my head moved back and forth. I couldn't stay still. "Mom," I said quietly, "I'm not staying here for the summer and I'm not moving to Surrey with you and Dad."

Mom stared at me, her eyebrows pulled together, her mouth open, as if I had spoken in a foreign language.

The Getaway

IF I WANTED to leave home, I would have to outwit Dad. Any hesitation on my part, any discussion, and he would use every one of his tactics to render me powerless and compliant. I imagined the sneer in his voice and the words he might use. "You think you're so smart, don't you? A real Miss Smarty-pants. Too good to help out your mother and me." He wouldn't stop.

I remembered the way he had talked to Sarah the one time she came home for a visit after her move to Calgary—probably the reason she hadn't been back since. On her first night home, she modeled her new black coat with a faux fur collar.

"Isn't it beautiful?" She laughed and twirled in the kitchen, pretending she was a model. "It's wool." The coat *was* beautiful, the fabric soft and luxurious in my fingers. With her blonde hair, she was stunning in it, and I was happy for her.

Dad lay in wait for four days before cornering her after supper on the last night of her five-day visit. We girls were doing the dishes. Janice, who preferred to wash, had her hands in the soapy water. I dried and Sarah put the dishes away in the cupboard. Dad stood in front of the woodstove with his arms across his chest and a toothpick in his fingers, one of his favorite positions. Mom had gone upstairs. The boys were in the living room. Dad suddenly made a loud, snorting noise. I jumped. We all turned around. My stomach dropped.

Dad's face twisted in disdain. He began to taunt Sarah just as he'd done when she lived at home. "You think you're better than us now, with your new coat and fancy clothes, do you? Prancing around with no thought for any of us here at home. How do you think you make your sisters feel with all your expensive gewgaws and finery?"

Panic rose inside me. Oh no, please, *Dad, not tonight, not on her last night here.* Sarah froze, a dish in her hand. Her face went white and her eyes huge. Her mouth half-opened. None of us made a sound. The air crackled with fear. Sarah started to cry. Deep, heartbroken sobs with the dish still in her hand. My heart hurt for her, while at the same time I was angry. I dropped the dish towel on the counter and took the stairs to my room. Janice stayed behind.

I'd wanted to warn Sarah, to hiss, "Don't let him bully you. Don't let him crush you again and again. Don't let him win." I'd been too afraid.

Later, after Dad left for a bishopric meeting, I heard Sarah sob to Mom in the downstairs hallway. "Why doesn't our family love each other the way families who aren't members of the church do?" I didn't hear Mom's reply.

Years before Sarah left home, I had determined never to let Dad talk to me the way he did to her. Even the thought of being the target of his rage made me sick. My best defence was to avoid him. Whenever he stared at me and narrowed his eyes, I disappeared. It was the only safe thing to do. I had never once heard him demean Janice, or even try.

After Mom told me she and Dad couldn't help me with university, I phoned Don. As soon as he heard my voice he asked, "Are you okay? You sound as if you're sick or something. Have you got a cold?"

"No, no, I don't have a cold. I'm upset." My voice broke.

"Oh no, what happened?"

"I've got to leave. I've got to leave as soon as I can. They're not going to help me go to Simon Fraser. They'll help Janice with university, but not me." I choked back sobs. "They want *me* to help *them* instead." Bitterness flooded me.

"Tell me what you want me to do. Do you want me to come over and pick you up right now?

"No, no, not yet."

"Are you sure? I can get in my car right now. I can't stand the thought of you in that house any longer."

"I've got to get a job and a place to live first."

"Promise me you'll call me if you change your mind."

The next day, a Wednesday, I took the transit bus into Vancouver. On the ride downtown, my heart hurt as my mind replayed the conversation with Mom about university. I had lain awake all night thinking about it and about Mom and Dad and about the church. The employment agency listed in the help-wanted section of the *Sun* was located in an office building on Granville Street. An old-fashioned elevator with a metal grid lifted me to the fifth floor. The office was down the corridor and around a corner. I clutched the folded newspaper in one hand, smoothed the skirt of my graduation dress, and turned the door handle.

A foyer with two folding chairs led onto a small room with a wooden desk stacked with manila folders and a scratched, metal filing cabinet. It reminded me of one of the office scenes in the movie *In the Heat of the Night* that Don and I had just seen. All that was missing were the half-dead flies and the overhead fan. Behind the desk sat a middle-aged woman wearing rhinestone glasses. Through the half-open window, soot and bird dung coated the gray bricks of the building next door. The woman smiled. "What ad are you here about?"

"Not any particular ad." I smiled my best smile. "I'm looking for a job in an office. A starter position. I've just graduated from high school."

Her smile faltered. "I'm sorry, dear, but all our clients want experienced secretaries." My legs weakened. Maybe I *should* find a waitressing job rather than try for something more. Then a silent voice prompted me to talk to her as if she was a friend.

"I've just started looking," I chirped. "Your agency is the first one I've tried. Thank goodness it's a sunny day out." My eyes glanced at the open window.

"Yes, the weather's warmed up, hasn't it? Sitting here talking on the phone all day, I'm thankful to have a window that opens.

Whew." She fanned her face with her hand.

"It's already boiling hot outside," I burbled on. "And not even noon yet. On the bus ride from Richmond, it was sweltering. It's hard to believe it's only the end of June." I was stronger now, more confident.

The woman lifted a pen from her desk, cocked her head, and squinted. "Can you type?"

"Yes, eighty words a minute. And I took bookkeeping too." My heart lifted.

She ran her tongue over her lips and rifled through a stack of papers. "Hmm, something came in that I don't usually handle. I was just about to file it away. Nothing fancy, mind you. A receptionist in the office of a lumber company. It's not much more than minimum wage, but it would give you office experience to build a resume with."

Albion Forest Products, a family-run business, was a short bus ride away on the corner of Hastings and Commercial. Inside, I smelled fresh-cut lumber and oily metal. An arrow directed me upstairs to the office. At the top was an empty reception desk with no one in sight. I cleared my throat and called out, "Hello?"

A plump, colorless woman peered around the door: Helen, the bookkeeper. "Come in, come in. Lana, our receptionist, is on her lunch break. She's probably out wedding shopping. She's about to get married, the reason she's leaving us."

The job involved answering a twelve-line telephone system, recording sales invoices, and typing letters. The family owned a second store, Lumberland, a few streets away on Powell Street.

As Helen explained the position, I glanced at the chips on the edge of her desk and the faded upholstery on the chair beside me. The carpet was worn and had a few stains. I didn't think they would be too picky about who they hired. I showed her my transcript from grade twelve and told her I couldn't afford to go to university—yet.

"With your grades and typing speed, I think you'll be able to do what we need. Can you start on Monday? That will give Lana a week to train you."

I've got a job, I've got a job, I sang to myself on the bus home to Richmond, tingling with nerves and excitement. I would have to keep it a secret from Mom and Dad. That morning before he left for work at the landfill, Dad had fixed me with a stern look and said, "I expect you to help your mother here. We've got a lot to do to get the house spruced up for sale." I kept my face impassive and didn't say anything, aware that as soon as he left, I was taking the bus into town to find a job.

On my walk home from the bus stop, I skipped and spun in circles. Mom was in the vegetable garden weeding. I stayed on the grass, careful not to get my shoes or dress dirty. "How was your day?" she asked as she stood up, brushing her gloved hands together and rubbing the small of her back. She wore her outside work clothes: tan baggy trousers, one of Dad's old plaid shirts loose over top, and a floppy sun hat. She sagged with weariness.

"I registered with an employment agency for office work. I'll change out of my clothes and come help you." She had a question in her eyes, but I wasn't about to tell her that I had found a job. She was sure to tell Dad.

"Guess what," I whispered over the phone later to Don. "Guess what. I found a job in an office today, a real office." I suppressed giggles.

"Already?"

"Yes, isn't that fabulous? I'm pinching myself."

"Wow, good for you. Where?"

"Albion Forest Products at Hastings and Commercial. It's just a job as a receptionist. I start on Monday. I can't tell Mom and Dad yet. I've got to find a place to live first." Leaving was becoming real. That night, after I finally dropped off to sleep, a dream woke me. In it Dad was shouting, "You can't leave. We need you here." When I tried to run, my legs were paralyzed.

The next day, Thursday, after Dad left for work, I changed into my school clothes and walked to the bus stop. My stomach was jumpy. I was sure Mom had told Dad I had been out job hunting yesterday. I half-expected him to be hiding in the truck parked behind some bushes, spying on me.

Downtown, I bought a *Sun* and circled the ads for shared houses, then found a telephone booth. A room in a house on 7th Avenue just east of Burrard Street was the most promising. I liked the house right away: yellow, an old-fashioned thirties-style, with wide front steps and a veranda, two blocks from the bus line on Broadway. Heart pounding, I walked up the steps and rang the bell. *Please let this be the right one.*

A woman in her twenties with short dark hair opened the door. She showed me around and chattered nonstop. Within minutes she told me her name was Anita, that she worked as a nurse at the Vancouver General close by, had an Italian boyfriend, was in charge of renting out the room, and her hair was short because it had all broken off when she had it colored. She was suing the hairdresser.

The space for rent was a shared upstairs bedroom with a view onto 7th Avenue and the car dealership across the street. The other bed was rented by a girl named Charlene, who was nineteen. "If you want to meet her, you'll have to come back after five-thirty when she gets home from work. I'm sure you'll get along fine. She's quiet and keeps to herself."

If I took it, I would have a single bed and half of the room-length closet. Six women shared the house. The bathroom was down the hall. I wouldn't have to pay for electricity or the telephone, except for long-distance calls. The kitchen was stocked with dishes and pots and pans. I could use the living room to watch television or invite friends over.

"I wouldn't wait too long to decide. The rent is reasonable for what you get. The ad went in today and I've already had a couple of calls. It's clean and safe in a good location. It won't last."

My stomach flip-flopped. The rent was a little over a third of my new salary. What if I hated the girl named Charlene? Yet if I waited and came back after five-thirty to meet her, the room might be gone. Anita was good-hearted even though she was pretty hyper. What about the other women in the house?

After I paid my first month's rent from my tuition and books money, I wanted to cry. I had just exchanged part of my future for a place to live. My life wasn't going to be the same as the rest of my friends from school. But then, my life had never been like theirs.

Back at home, I called Don. My voice shook as I whispered, "I've found a place. I hope I've done the right thing."

"Don't worry. If it doesn't work out, at least you'll be away from home and you can find something better." I clung to his voice.

"Do you think you could get off work a little bit earlier tomorrow and help me move before Dad gets home? And stop at the grocery store and get me four or five cardboard boxes?"

The next morning, Friday, as Dad opened the kitchen door to go out to the truck, his battered lunch kit in his hand, I grabbed hold of the back of a chair. Over the thumping of my heart, I mentioned as casually as I could, "Mom's probably told you I've registered with an employment agency. I plan to work in an office and share a house with other girls in Vancouver."

Dad's hand locked onto the door knob. I turned and walked purposefully down the hall and up the stairs to my bedroom, closed my door, and shook. I expected to hear Dad's footsteps pounding up the stairs. They never came. After the pickup bumped over the bridge onto the road, I talked to Mom. I had to make my getaway before Dad came home from work at six o'clock. We sat across from each other at the kitchen table, just as we had at the start of the week. On that day, I was excited about going to university. Now, everything was different.

"I found a job." My voice was determined. "I start on Monday as a receptionist in the office of a building supply store. I've rented a room in Vancouver in a house with five other women. Don is coming over to help me move in the afternoon."

Mom dabbed away tears with the bottom of her apron. She appeared to age ten years. For a moment, I was sorry for her, then my resolve hardened. She finally spoke. "I wish you'd change your mind and stay. Take some time to think things through a little more."

"Think things through to what, Mom? You and Dad are moving to Surrey. What is there for me? I've got to make a life for myself."

Mom blinked and swallowed as if she was in pain. "There's a nice church congregation in Surrey with lots of young people. I'm sure you'll make new friends right away, the same as you did when we moved here."

"Mom." My body shook. "I'm moving into Vancouver." There was no point in getting into another argument with her about the church.

"Your father's not going to be happy. We'll miss you."

Don was coming to pick me up just after four o'clock. I had to be packed and gone before Dad got home. I would have less than two hours. Every time the phone rang my chest tightened. What if it was Dad? Had Mom called and left a message with somebody in the shed at the landfill? What if he left work and came home early? When he found out I was really leaving, he was sure to be mad, steaming mad, and primed for a blowup.

What should I take? All my belongings were piled on my bed. Clothes, shoes, school records, a few church-approved fiction books, my toiletries, Rob's black Elphinstone High cardigan, and a glossy picture book of Grimm's Fairy Tales, an award for good citizenship in grade one.

Don arrived at four-fifteen. His smile was strained as he passed me six flattened cardboard boxes and said hello to Mom. She glared at him. "Uh," he said, glancing away from her and over at me. "I'll wait outside until you're ready." I folded the boxes together and threw my belongings into them, my ears tuned for the engine of Dad's pickup. At five o'clock Don stacked the boxes on the back seat of his Chev.

Leaving was surreal. Relief mixed with regret overwhelmed me.

I was terrified of what lay ahead, yet if I wanted a life of honesty and choice, I couldn't stay. Desperation and determination pushed me forward. Mom and Dad were chattels of the LDS church, with all hope of wholeness obliterated by the legacy of Joseph Smith. They were each stunted in different ways. I had lived a lie to stay safe from them my whole life. I couldn't lie anymore. My choice to leave home was no choice at all. It was inevitable, years in coming, yet my decision to go, to find a job and a place to live, had happened within four days. Don drove out the driveway and turned onto River Road. I didn't look back.

The Trickster

I WENT TO SLEEP each night serenaded by voices and laughter from the kitchen downstairs. Playing cards snapped on the Arborite table and the smell of pizza wafted up the stairs. Doors opened and closed gently against the mellow tunes of the Poppy Family on the record player in the living room. Everything was new and strange and wonderful. Yet every so often, anxiety out of nowhere doubled me over and left me gasping.

My roommates, between the ages of nineteen and twenty-six, weren't Mormon. None of them went to any church. They smoked, drank, and talked about sex, all taboo for Mormons. I watched them as a tourist might: how they dressed, whether they stayed overnight with their boyfriends, and what they said about their families. Charlene, whom I shared a bedroom with, turned out to be as quiet and agreeable as Anita had promised.

The night after I moved in, one of my roommates, incredulous, asked, "You mean you've never played cards? Oh come on, you must have played something, sometime." I shook my head and didn't tell her it was forbidden by the church. I didn't tell any of my roommates that my parents were Mormon and that I was baptized too. I wanted to be normal, to be a part of the world they lived in, not the shameful one I had come from. They taught me how to play crazy eights and rummy, and laughed at my feeble attempts to learn how to shuffle cards. In their fingers, the cards were a blur.

After my alarm jolted me awake, I stood at the kitchen counter, ate a bowl of cereal and milk, then pulled out one of the sandwiches from the freezer I had made ahead—store-bought bread and a piece of bologna, spread with French's mustard and wrapped in wax paper. I walked the two blocks to the bus stop on Broadway at Burrard.

My job was easy to learn. Lana, the receptionist who was supposed to train me, spent her last week at work admiring her diamond ring and talking about her wedding. "See those clear buttons on the phone," she said, pointing with a pink, lacquered nail when I came in the first Monday. "When one of those lights up, pick up the receiver, push in the button, say 'Albion Forest Products. How may I direct your call?' and then push the extension the caller asks for. When you hear a voice answer, hang up. They can't hear you, so if you want to stay on the line and listen, you can."

After the first few calls, I relaxed. Recording the sales invoices, the other part of the job, involved entering numbers in columns in a ledger and adding them up on an adding machine. By the end of the afternoon, I was a mindless machine myself.

Don usually picked me up after supper. We'd saunter, hand in hand in the sticky summer heat, through the streets of Vancouver's West End close to Stanley Park. Sometimes we watched a movie in the air-conditioned darkness of a theater on Granville Street: *The Graduate*, *Bonny and Clyde*, *Guess Who's Coming to Dinner*.

On weekends, he cooked me spaghetti and garlic bread or pork chops and mashed potatoes at his apartment on Comox Street. The intimacies we shared afterward were new and exciting at first but quickly became boring and routine, as their focus was on pleasing Don. They didn't stir an erotic charge or any satisfaction for me. I didn't have the life experience to recognize that Don wasn't a playful or sensual person. I craved both, yet was unaware that that's what was missing.

A glance from Charles, a smile, the lift of an eyebrow had left me breathless. That didn't happen with Don, yet I didn't realize that Don and I were completely mismatched. Although the church's prohibition against necking and sex before marriage was irrelevant to me now, I was always back at the house well before midnight.

Don steadied me. The knowledge that he was a phone call

away, that there was someone who cared about me for whom I didn't have to be a Mormon, was comforting. He was supportive of me in the same way Rob and Sarah had been, and I was grateful to him. But I didn't understand that grateful wasn't a foundation for choosing a life partner, or that attaching myself to another person's life before I had figured out my own couldn't fill the empty spaces inside me and make me whole.

Mom visited me once but wouldn't come inside. She parked on the street in front of the house and waited until I came out to the station wagon. Before her visit, tense and nervous, I hid my roommates' empty beer bottles on the back porch. If she had come inside, she would have smelled their cigarette smoke. The evening was warm and muggy, the air heavy as if a thunderstorm was closing in. I trudged down the steps to the car and got in. She'd brought me leaf lettuce from the garden, washed, in a plastic bag, and a hard-covered church book.

"Do you have everything you need?"

"I'm fine, Mom, I'm fine." There was no use talking to her about my bitterness over working at a repetitive, meaningless job because I hadn't had the confidence to figure out how to go to university without her and Dad as a backup. I was awkward and uncomfortable on the seat beside her, sure that the people walking by could hear what she was saying through the open windows.

"You could easily go to church services at the Vancouver ward on 41st. I'm sure one of the members would even come and pick you up. Think about it." There wasn't anything to think about. I didn't have a testimony of the gospel. Taking the book Mom brought was easier than thrusting it back at her and seeing the hurt in her eyes. I refused, however, to do more than glance at it because Joseph Smith's name was on the cover. The book was a symbol of all that I had missed out on in life. It represented the reason I'd left home. It was the opposite of everything I wanted: the freedom to make my own choices and be a real person, not a mindless robot following LDS rules, afraid to say what I thought. Mom's offer of a church book was her idea of love. Back in the house, I angrily shoved it out of sight in my closet.

I didn't think about Dad, other than being relieved to be away from him. I was different than anyone in my family, although I had never been able to figure out exactly why. None of my family questioned or asked for an explanation about anything that I thought was important in life. They meekly accepted and obeyed. I was curious about how the world worked, why people did what they did, and different ways of thinking.

Mormon doctrine said that as spirits, we lived in a pre-existence and chose our parents. We came to earth so we could prove ourselves worthy, by doing good works, to go on to eternal progression in heaven. I thought my life better fit the theory of reincarnation I had learned about at school—suffering today for something I had done wrong in a previous lifetime.

On Saturdays, I visited the downtown Vancouver Public Library. It was cheaper than buying books and another way to save money. One afternoon, after checking out three novels for the week, I wandered around the library and stumbled upon a section on religion. I was surprised at the number of books. Instant anger at the church and Mom and Dad bubbled up. I wheeled away but a small voice said, "Stop!" I glanced around. There was no one behind me. Eeriness shivered through me. Then I felt light, as if I was floating. My eyes went to the line of books on the shelves. The spine of one caught my attention and my hand reached for it, as if propelled by an unseen force.

The book I pulled off the shelf was *No Man Knows My History: The Life of Joseph Smith*, written by Fawn Brodie. I flipped through the table of contents. Stunned, I lay my purse and novels on the floor by my feet. *No Man Knows My History* wasn't one of the books on Mom and Dad's bookshelf at home.

My eyes scanned each page. I barely breathed. The rustle of pages turning and the muffled coughs around me fell away. What I read was unbelievable, yet everything was documented, with specific references to journals and diaries, personal letters, legal transcripts, court documents, and newspaper articles. I went into a trance. The thump of books brought me back to the library. A glance at the clock told me it was closing time. I burned to read on but the book was reference only. I replaced it reluctantly.

While I refused to give attention to the scriptures of the church, blocking them out at services and in classes where I filed my nails, I had absorbed the story of the church through every pore. A chronic virus, it was a part of me. I grew up hearing it over and over. "As a young farm boy of fourteen, Joseph Smith went into the woods to pray and asked God which church to join . . . God appeared to him and told him not to join any of them but to start his own . . ."

Fawn Brodie's book told a different story. In the following week, bits and pieces of what I had read churned in an endless loop in my mind. Betrayal and outrage roared inside me. The church Mom and Dad bowed down to, and had neglected our family for, was based on lie after lie. I wanted to scream until I had no voice left and pound my fists on something hard, all to make the pain and anger go away. The life I had been forced to live was based on a hoax, a made-up story, all lies. None of it was real.

The next Saturday, I was at the library as soon as it opened. The book was still there. I grabbed it and sat down at one of the tables. The scrape of a chair being pulled out and the crackle of a newspaper annoyed me, then ceased to matter. According to Fawn Brodie and the historians she referenced, Joseph Smith was a treasure hunter, fascinated with magic and the occult. He wasn't praying in the forest when he was fourteen, he was in trouble with the law. As an adult, he wrote the story about finding secret gold plates with the Mormon scriptures on them: gold plates that were so powerful he couldn't show them to anyone. If ordinary men viewed them, they'd be instantly struck dead.

I stuffed down hysteria. My ancestors had believed his ruse and Mom and Dad did too. I'd never given it much thought—it was just part of the story of the church I grew up with. It was so obviously a ridiculous charade, it was laughable.

The prophet Mom and Dad worshipped had delusions of becoming a god of the world. I wasn't aware that he'd run for president of the United States and been defeated. Or that he'd had visions of a sovereign Mormon state, selected a council of fifty princes to form the highest court on earth, and had himself crowned king of the Kingdom of God.

Horror flooded me. I read the passages again and again, made a visit to the women's washroom, stood outside on the library steps and ate an apple, then went back inside. A woman's voice over the loudspeaker pulled me back to the present: "The library is closing in ten minutes."

The next Saturday I chose another reference book, *Mormonism: A Study of Mormon History and Doctrine* by Jerald and Sandra Tanner, and two more thick books on religion that had sections about the early days of the Mormons. The authors, including Fawn Brodie, were scholars and professors, former Mormons excommunicated by the church for publishing their research on the history and doctrine of the religion.

My eyes hurt and I had a headache from reading, yet I couldn't stop. I frantically read back and forth, comparing sections and references in each of the books. With each new discovery, as my upbringing collided with reality, I became more off-balance and woozy. Joseph Smith was a thief and a con man, a convicted criminal. He had a militia that burned, pillaged, and murdered. His secret police, the Destroying Angels, carried out executions. I understood now why anything I had read growing up was censored by Mom and Dad. In the story that the church put out, Joseph Smith died a martyr for his religious beliefs. In the accounts I read, he died with a gun in his hand in a shoot-out, after he burned a printing press, while the family of a young girl he'd had sex with was after him.

I wondered whether Mom was familiar with any of what I'd read at the library. I thought maybe she wasn't, but even if she was, I doubted that it would make any difference to her loyalty or that of Dad's to the church. There was no use trying to talk to her about what I had discovered. If she knew, she had accepted it. If she didn't, she would never believe me or anything written in the books at the library, no matter how many historical records supported it.

The books I read contained pictures of Joseph Smith that weren't included in any church literature I had ever seen. He resembled a fox. His wide forehead tapered to a long, narrow chin. His mouth was petulant and weak. But it was the penetrating, blank stare in his eyes that raised my biliousness. His eyes were devoid of light.

It was at the library that I gained my testimony of the gospel. I was convinced that Joseph Smith was a trickster, a man who did and said without conscience whatever was necessary to satisfy his insatiable appetite for wealth, power, and sex. His made-up stories, his lies, and his actions had hurt people and destroyed families, both during his lifetime and in the church generations that followed. The lives of my ancestors, my parents, and my brothers and sisters had been devoured by his magic tricks and self-serving rhetoric.

On the third Saturday, at home after my visit to the library, I marched up the stairs to my bedroom. There was one last thing I needed to do to confirm my new-found testimony of the LDS church and claim my life as my own. From the back of my closet, I dug out the book on Mormonism that Mom had given me and chucked it into the garbage.

End-run - 2004

WITH DAD'S FUNERAL safely over, I decide to take a drive past the rock bluff and the entrance to Mom and Dad's ranch on Valley View Road in Penticton. There are view homes on the rock now, the first time I've seen them, and the ranch, worth millions, is in the name of a stranger—my youngest brother. I turn around in the parking lot of Skaha Bluffs Provincial Park and drive back down the hill in the summer heat.

Mom and Dad came a long way after they fed us food from the garbage dump. They bought and sold property in Surrey, then purchased an orchard on Valley View Road. After subdividing, they still owned a sixty-four-acre ranch and a fifteen-acre rock bluff, both with a view of Skaha Lake.

Only my oldest and youngest brothers remained active LDS members with Mom and Dad. Over the years, the rest of my siblings confronted their own crises of faith and followed me out of the church. They kept their reasons to themselves. Distance that couldn't be measured in miles separated us.

Every seven or eight years, the Mormons and non-Mormons and all our kids would meet up at the ranch for a two-day reunion, the only time we all saw each other. Scattered throughout Canada and the United States, every member of my family called the ranch home. As tenuous as it was, the need within us for family was still there. We rode horses, picked cherries, and tubed down the Penticton River Channel. On Sunday, the Mormons would go to church and Mom would try to persuade the non-Mormons to attend. The spirit we had shared as a family for less than forty-eight hours would evaporate. It was the signal to pack up and leave.

Dad was the bishop in the Penticton ward, the honored king of his congregation. At our reunions Mom would reiterate, "The reason we moved here was so Dad could be the bishop." He was generous with his church family in a way he never was with his own children. He would guarantee loans and mortgages for members, with the ranch as collateral. One of the members he guaranteed a mortgage for was convicted of having sex with his daughter and sent to prison. Another never paid him back the $40,000 he loaned for a natural food store.

The ranch was home and heart to me. For two days every seven or eight years, I had a family to share with my children. I took what I could get. The property accomplished what Mom, Dad, and the church hadn't. The ranch was an anchor in my life, offering unconditional love, giving and asking nothing in return.

Then, in the late 1990s while Dad was in negotiations with a developer for the sale of the ranch, he was diagnosed with dementia. Mom followed the church's advice to aging members and liquidated their assets. It was a simple yet brilliant cash cow for the church, reaping one-tenth in tithing on any increase. It missed out, however, on its due from the value of the ranch and the rock bluff.

In her eighties by this time, Mom secretly signed over the ranch to my brother Peter. He was the youngest in the family by seven years and hadn't known the hunger and shame the rest of us were raised on. He lived in Penticton and whispered want into Mom's ear, daily. She kept her checkbook handy for his benefit. On one of Dad's good mornings, Peter drove Mom and Dad to a notary public in downtown Penticton to sign over the title. None of them mentioned the transfer to the rest of the family. As a Mormon, Peter had been well schooled by the church and Mom and Dad in keeping secrets. Dad believed he still owned the ranch. Mom and Dad moved down the hill to a house on Main Street, close to the LDS chapel.

Without consulting the rest of the family, and with Mom's approval, Peter arranged a private sale of the rock bluff to a neighbor for a token payment. Another secret. Again, on one of Dad's good days, Peter drove Mom and Dad to the notary to sign over the title. I had never thought Peter was very bright, yet he was clever enough to outsmart his six siblings and their children—and steal any inheritance. Everything Mom and Dad had worked for while we kids did without was gone.

One by one, my siblings and I discovered that we'd been excluded from the decision making and from a share in the properties. Heartache ricocheted over the telephone. With the secret transfer of the properties, the thread holding our family together had snapped. We talked bitterly about a lawsuit but discovered that it would involve a civil court case against the notary public, Peter, and Mom. With Mom taking care of Dad and her own health failing, none of us was willing to cause her distress.

Did Mom understand the impact of her actions? Did it matter to her? Her church family supported her in her decisions. They were the ones she consulted, not her children. They all knew Peter and claimed him as one of their own. Rob, although still a Mormon, was invisible in Idaho. He was as hurt as the rest of us. Janice, well set financially, was the only sibling I never heard express any emotion. I buried my hurt under anger. What made me think I was entitled to, or could expect, transparency and fairness? Arrgh. Would I never learn? Mom was still in a bubble where nothing made sense. Her loyalty was to the church and her church family.

I talked to Mom on the phone. "What about the rest of us? There was plenty to share among all us kids."

"I thought Peter and his wife needed the ranch for their self-esteem. And the neighbors wanted the fifteen acres as a place for their relatives to stay when they hike Skaha Bluffs."

I asked Peter, "What about your brothers and sisters? Weren't we important to you as family?"

"Mom wanted me to have the ranch. It wasn't up to me to tell anyone about it. If Mom and Dad wanted you to know, they would have told you." By this time, Dad couldn't remember how to find the kitchen.

"What about the fifteen acres?" Homes made of concrete and

glass, with a panoramic view of the lake, perched on the rock.

"I didn't think they were worth anything."

Pain seared through me. His words paralleled Mom and Dad's treatment of our family. The church's slogan of families first was another lie among the many I was raised with. Rather than strengthening our family's bonds, LDS doctrine and Mom and Dad's mindless loyalty to it destroyed them.

Exodus – 2010

MOM SEES ME in the doorway. "My Maggie girl," she wheezes. Happiness lights up her eyes. Her frail body is a small mound under the blankets. Her eyes are huge in her pale, sunken face.

Mom's room at Trinity Care Home in Penticton is air-conditioned and filled with the scent of roses. I could be in a comfortable hotel room, except for the wheelchair and oxygen tank. One wall is lined with family photos. A picture of the Salt Lake City temple is smack in the middle. I sit beside her hospital bed and clasp her blue-veined hand in mine. My heart squeezes with love.

I stopped at the reception desk in the foyer when I came in and talked to the nurse on duty. Her voice was gentle. "She could pass anytime. It's her heart. All we can do now is to keep her comfortable and manage her pain. People choose their own time. When she's ready, she'll go."

Mom has been prepared for years. When Dad died six years ago, she had me drive her to Everden Rust funeral home to show me the casket she'd chosen. "This is the one." Mom pointed to a fancy blue casket with the lid raised. Her voice filled with pleasure, as if she was talking about a dress or a coat. "I've ordered it in white." She ran her fingers lightly over the satin lining, then rested her hand on the lid, reluctant to leave.

I kept my face blank. For her, the white coffin was a symbol of divinity, everything she'd worked and sacrificed for her entire life. "How nice," I murmured, recognizing what the coffin represented, yet thinking, How can she look forward to being closed inside such a small space with the lid shut tight on top of her? My lungs gasped at the thought.

Mom had no choice about a casket. The church frowns on cremation. A natural green burial isn't acceptable either. She believes she'll be resurrected, her body raised up in the same form as on earth, so she needs to keep it intact. I didn't ask her what age she believes she'll be when she's resurrected. I vaguely remember hearing different answers growing up. Better to stay away from any discussion about Mormon doctrine.

Alone with Mom at Trinity, I'm grateful there are no brothers or sisters here to shove me out of the way or vie to be the most attentive. I'm relieved, too, that she recognized me. It was only the once that she didn't, but I've never been able to trust that it won't happen again. One day in the 1980s when I walked in the door of the farmhouse at the ranch, she waited to be introduced to me. It was the first time she'd seen me on my own, not clinging to the arm of a husband, since I was eighteen years old. If I'd had my three children with me, the kids would have been a sure identifier.

"I can't believe it's you." Mom had laughed with embarrassment. "You look too young." The difference she noticed went beyond the capris and t-shirt that hugged the curves of my newly slim body. I had finally made it to Simon Fraser University and was living my own dream.

On the table beside Mom's bed, a Zeller's flyer, open to a sale on pots and pans, teeters on a stack of church books and slides onto her bed. "Plan on going shopping?" I smile and lean in close to retrieve it.

"I might just need those if I ever get back into a house of my own," Mom whispers. Her voice is stronger than when I first came in. Her eyes are serious and fixed on me. The fingers of her right hand fret with the top edge of the soft blanket over her chest. I glance up at the metal monster suspended from the ceiling above the bed. The contraption with pulleys and a sling is used to lift her body, ravaged by osteoporosis, from the bed into her wheelchair. She isn't going anywhere.

There's little I can do to make her more comfortable. Tuck the blankets closer around her neck? She hates to be cold. Retie the dangling strings of the standard-issue gown she's wearing? With a warm cloth dampened in the ensuite sink, I stroke the fine parchment of her face, arms, and hands, more gently than I would for an infant. I remember as a child laying a dampened cloth on her forehead when she had one of her migraines. I run a comb with delicate care through what's left of her angel-fine white hair. She tries to smile.

The staff hover, appearing in the doorway every so often as I'm tending Mom. A fresh-faced young aide with short curly hair asks, "Are you sure you don't want something stronger for the pain, dear?"

Mom moves her head no. "The morphine gives me nightmares. I'll stick to the Tylenol."

"If you change your mind, just buzz."

It won't be long before she's free of pain. I hope it's soon. It hurts to see her suffer. The labor of going out of the world, like birth, can't be hurried. When she dies, I'll be free of the expectations she had for me and the weight of her disappointment. We'll both be at peace.

"Can you reach that glass for me, dear? I'm so thirsty." Mom's voice is back to a wheeze. I hold the straw to her mouth. She manages a sip, barely enough to moisten her lips.

What does Mom need before she *can* let go? I have no idea what the landscape of her inner life is, although she was lonely after Dad died. Does she have any regrets about her life? Is there someone she wants to see? The language of feelings and needs isn't part of her vocabulary. Duty and obedience are.

Mom was never interested in knowing what I thought or felt as a child, nor does she know the woman I've grown into. The church is what she prizes above all else. I'm one of her sorrows, an embarrassment she's had to explain to her church family.

On a summer visit to Penticton a few years ago, I reconnected with my high school friend Sandy, who had moved to the Okanagan town. "When I chatted with your mom after my move," Sandy told me, "she told me not to believe everything you said."

"Mom said w-h-a-t?"

"She made out that you were missing a few marbles, if you get my drift." Sandy laughed, rolled her eyes, and shook her head. "I like your mom. She's always been kind to me, even though I left the church after I moved here, but I'm sure glad I don't have her for a mother."

Sandy's validation of my experience of Mom affirmed my reality. Mom considers me the troublemaker in the family. She uses the church's yardstick to define me. According to Mom, which means the church, there *is* something wrong with me. Besides leaving the church, I challenged its patriarchal structure by speaking openly about what went on in our family. I'm the only one who did.

I shift on the chair beside Mom and readjust my hands on hers. I know she expects that her obedience to the church will reap rewards in Mormon heaven when she dies: returning to live with God, whom she calls her Heavenly Father; joining Dad, who is supposedly a god now, with his own worlds to rule over; and continuing to procreate with him as one of his multiple heavenly wives . . .

I think of her in her wheelchair in the bishop's office in Penticton after Dad died. She was expected to settle up with the church for Dad's tithing and offerings. In sickness and death, the church still has its hand out. When Mom dies, there will be no one to write the checks. Impotent triumph surges through me.

Does Mom picture Dad with his arms outstretched in joy, waiting on the other side to welcome her with love? I never saw him do that while he was alive. I read in Dad's journal that after he left on his mission, while Mom waited for him, he fell in love with Pearl, a missionary he met in Salt Lake City. He wrote to her and asked her to marry him. She never replied. Is Mom aware she was Dad's second choice?

Sitting beside Mom's bed with her hands in mine, it occurs to me that her life as a woman couldn't have been fulfilling, in the way I gauge fulfillment. Growing up, we kids were her confidants. There were times when her need was a mass of slithering tentacles, wrapping themselves around me to feed.

"Will you give me one of those therapeutic touch treatments you told me you were learning to do?" Mom's daring, asking me for something that the church considers evil, surprises me. Only men who hold the priesthood are believed to have access to God's healing power. Maybe she's past caring about anything but her pain. Is she afraid of dying?

I hold her paper-thin hands in mine, close my eyes, and imagine myself surrounded by white light. *Please let me be a conduit for healing energy to ease Mom's pain.* I open my eyes and move my hands, palms down, a few inches above her body. My hands warm, sensing heavy areas around her. With gentle movements I clear them away. My lips brush Mom's forehead and cheek. My hands cradle hers. Her face is relaxed and drowsy. Love flows from my heart to hers and back, expanding to fill the room and beyond. Waves of bliss hum through me. My love is enough for both of us.

My own losses and pain fall away. I am weightless and fluid. For the first time in my life, there is no church talk from Mom, no preaching or judgment, no hurt. Just Mom and me, surrounded by a love so strong and pure that the power of the Mormon church can't enter in. God is here with us and we are with God.

The Family Today

Rob has passed away. His surviving wife, their three children, and their families live in various cities in the United States. They remain active members of the church.

Sarah and her second husband live in Oregon. Neither she nor her husband or any of her four children or their families are practicing members of the church.

Janice and her second husband live in British Columbia. Neither she nor her husband or daughter are practicing members of the church.

Maggie lives in British Columbia. Neither she nor her three children or granddaughters are practicing members of the church.

Michael and his second wife live in British Columbia. He and his wife, as well as his three children and their families, all attend the Christian Alliance Church.

Ian is a street person and lives in Alberta. He is not a practicing member of the church.

Peter and his wife live in British Columbia. They remain active members of the church. Their children do not.

With Special Thanks

To

My brother Rob, who encouraged me to begin my story, even though we both knew he wasn't likely to agree with what I wrote about the Mormon church.

My sister Sarah, who shared her memories and confirmed mine.

My "writerly" friend Alexandra Amor, who encouraged me throughout my writing journey.

My beloved writing family of Scribblers.

My online writing group.

Bowen Island and my treasured heart family there.

My editor Joyce Gram, who gave me the permission I needed to write my childhood story without restraint. Thank you, Joyce, for reaffirming that I'm an adult now with a voice of my own.

The Author

Maggie Rayner lives on the West Coast of British Columbia, with a view of the ocean. She often visits Gibsons. Sailing, biking, and hiking endure as passions. Creating beautiful interiors for herself and others is a dream realized.

For further information visit the website www.maggierayner.com.